ACKNOWLEDGMENTS

My heartfelt thanks go to:

The Practitioner Certification class of the NLP Institute of California (Sunnyvale), 1996-1997 for "raising the bar" on the standards for learning and practicing NLP and requiring me to do the same as one of their coaches. Notably among them: Ed and Myra Hubbard, Rick Matthew, Joe Davis, Nan Crawford, Tom Huber, Janice Lum, Lisa Thompson, Myra Beals and Gina Rae Hendrickson.

For their unconditional support and friendship: Tracy Meisel, Wayne Evans, Christina Evans, Mike and Lisa Sloat, Jil Windsor and Craig Carr, Reuben Wolff, Dr. Kay Stewart, Tom Tshontikidis and Dexie Jean Campbell.

Jamie Walters, who took time out of her very busy life to edit this manuscript and who has been a constant source of encouragement, humor and darned good advice. Her work made this book eminently more useable, readable and enjoyable.

And most of all, my high school sweetheart, my best friend and my husband, Clifford Knox Campbell, for his unwavering belief in my ability to be a writer and for still being the coolest guy in class.

CHAPTER 1

INTRODUCTION

The Journey

Over the course of many years of studying philosophy, religion and mythology, it has become clear to me, on a very personal level, that stories have the power to enchant, transform, teach, and to connect in a systematic way the seemingly unrelated elements in a complex and confusing universe. Stories are a way of not just learning information, but of gaining wisdom.

It was while studying Neurolinguistic Programming (NLP) and hypnotherapy that I realized they had the same ability. Both rely on the artful use of language to refocus attention so that the subconscious can learn on a deeper level, unhindered by the critical mind.

The rising popularity and mainstream acceptance of NLP and hypnotherapy as healing art forms has occurred at the same time as renewed interest in mythology. Both NLP and hypnotherapy rely heavily on the use of language and communication at a subconscious level to teach, heal and effect profound personal change. It is these twin streams that have led me toward the vast ocean of storytelling, where most of the interesting stuff happens below the surface.

Personal Mythology

I believe that everyone has the potential to be a writer of mythology. Our everyday lives are a gold mine of material ready for the taking by anyone who is willing to devote some careful attention to their environment, and to spend a little time learning and practicing the basic elements of good storytelling. In fact, we tell our stories to the world every day by how we act, speak and otherwise express ourselves in the world. The question we should be asking ourselves is, "Who has written my myth?"

Many of us are walking around with myths that are outdated. Our cosmology has changed, but our myth hasn't changed to keep pace. I propose that the story of our lives is ongoing, subject to updating, revision and editing. As we gain new skills, insights and resources, we should invest the time to integrate these into our identity.

NLP and Storytelling

The ancient art of storytelling lends itself well to the learning and performing of NLP processes. It is an effective vehicle to deliver messages to the subconscious where the "aha's" of metaphor take place. It is our ability to make metaphorical connections that allows us to learn anything at all. When something new is like something we've done before, we take what we know from the first situation and transfer our knowledge to the new situation. In NLP terms, we take resources from a prior context and transfer them to the new context, taking us from present (or problem) state to desired state.

For its part, NLP gives back to the art of storytelling as well. With its emphasis on sensory-based communication, it can be used to enliven and enrich stories with details that appeal to all five senses. NLP's facility at effecting positive change makes it a powerful tool for updating the myths we live in the world.

Conscious resistance to being lectured, being burdened with "shoulds" and "have tos" give way to engaging in an activity that for thousands of years has brought people together to sit around a glowing object - be it a fire or a television - and form community. We still have the same basic physiology of our ancestors, and we still respond to the same archetypical imagery. The continuing popularity of Joseph Campbell's work, which many talented writers and researchers have used as a foundation, demonstrates that interest in mythology shows no signs of abating any time soon.

The Purpose of This Book

This book is designed to provide an alternative way to learn and deliver some of the basic concepts and processes of NLP. I do this for all those people whose learning styles are not supported by sitting in a windowless, air-conditioned room for eight hours at a time, going over each step of an NLP process in agonizing detail. It is also my sincere wish that readers will be inspired to look at their own lives as a rich source of material for creating their own myths, fables, folklore and stories.

This book will provide examples of my own stories wrapped around NLP processes, along with instructions and encouragement for you to try your own. No matter who your intended

The Well Formed Story
(How to Use NLP Processses in a Fictional Format)

By

Mary Shannon Campbell

Published by:
Meta*Force
e-mail: maryshannon@value.net

Library of Congress Catalog Card Number: 97-94427

ISBN: 0-9660177-0-6

Printed in the United States

TABLE OF CONTENTS

audience[1] is, you will reap enormous benefits as the storyteller.

I have discovered, to my delight, that the imagining, writing and telling of these stories has given me a deeper understanding of the discipline of NLP and also some unexpected and pleasant shifts in my own consciousness and way of operating in the world.

How to Use this Book

This is a workbook and therefore designed to be interactive. Don't just read it. Write in it. Draw in it. Paste pictures in it. Dance with it. Sing to it. Make notes in the margins. Get crazy. Color outside the lines.

The chapters about NLP processes have the same basic format: (1) the steps of the process is briefly summarized; (2) the purpose of the process is summarized; (3) each step is discussed in the context of fictional treatment; (4) two example stories are provided for each process; and (5) a Recap of Story worksheet is provided to give you the opportunity to write down which parts of the story you think fulfill each step of the NLP process.

I recap the stories to explain my use of fictional techniques in Chapter 17. My explanations, however, are by no means definitive, and some of my stories may vary from the precise structure of the processes. I freely admit to taking literary license and I encourage you to do the same.

The vast expanse of human history is open to you, as are all the genres of literature. Challenge yourself. Push back the barriers to your creativity and consider what it would be like to put an embedded NLP process in any one of the following genres:

- Science fiction.
- American western.
- Gothic romance.
- Murder mystery.
- Horror.
- Spy thriller.
- Travel adventure.

_____

[1]Throughout this work, I use the word "audience" to mean, interchangeably, yourself, a client or anyone else to whom a story is offered, either written or oral.

Flexibility is the key, along with a profound respect for the intelligence of your audience.

There is a Glossary of Terms in Chapter 15 to assist those who may not be familiar with NLP language. I have also taken the extraordinary liberty of re-wording the NLP Presuppositions in Chapter 16 to reflect the special needs and concerns of writers and storytellers.

Please note that the "Summary of the Process" sections in each chapter are just that: summaries, and very brief ones at that. I do not attempt to explain each process in great detail or provide instructions on doing the actual process as a direct form of intervention. In fact, some steps that may be included in a direct intervention are deliberately omitted in order to facilitate the process of giving fictional treatment to the processes. Many fine books already provide excellent examples of how to do direct NLP interventions. My intent is to provide a brief overview of each process so that it can be discussed in the context of storytelling.

As with any application of NLP, attention must be given to rapport and ecology. You should use your sensory acuity and flexibility to make any necessary adjustments in your delivery, style and content.

In addition, before you attempt to deliver an NLP process embedded in a story, please be certain that you have taken the necessary steps to arrive at a well-formed outcome. This is discussed in greater detail in Chapter 4.

Thank you for joining me on this adventure. You will find that I offer more questions than answers, and I encourage you to use the techniques in this book to:

-learn NLP on a deep level by weaving the principles and the steps of each process into enchanting tales;

-resolve issues that have been unaffected by direct application of NLP interventions;

-become more at ease with the conversational use of metaphor and NLP;

-offer stories to friends, loved ones and clients as gifts of insight, healing and transformation.

Chapter 2

CREATIVITY WARM-UPS

What used to be known as "Blank Page Syndrome" could now be called "Blank Screen Syndrome." Many of us dread sitting down to a blank writing surface. The following creativity exercises help alleviate the fear of writing and get your brain warmed up and ready to go.

In addition to limbering up your verbal skills, these exercises will shake you out of your comfort zone when it comes to how you perceive and use language. We can fall into a rut with our language, just like everything else. For proof, just flip through a dictionary and notice all the words you never use. They're yours, you know, free for the taking. Use these warm-ups to stretch your boundaries a little and expand into new linguistic territory.

Each exercise is designed to produce at least three sentences that have unique word combinations or characters doing unusual activities. After completing the exercises, use each of your new sentences to begin a short paragraph. If one particularly sparks your imagination, keep going. Write a page, two pages, a whole story.

You will notice that I put time limits on each exercise. This is a good way to condition your mind to produce within a specific time period. If you give yourself all the time in the world to write something, that is exactly how long it will take you. You never know when you might be called upon to create a story or a metaphor on the spot. Timing yourself in low risk situations, such as these exercises, is great practice. So, set that stop watch or egg timer and have some fun!

After each of the letters on the worksheet provided on page 13[2], write a word that starts with that letter. Let it be the first one that pops into your head. Don't try to think about it too hard; just relax and let them flow.

Example:

A	**alabaster**
B	**bearcat**
C	**camping**
D	**diamond**
E	**easy**
F	**forlorn**
G	**granola**
H	**hibernate**
I	**inch**
J	**jack**
K	**Kleenex**
L	**laughter**
M	**mountain**
N	**nowhere**
O	**oxymoron**
P	**pale**
Q	**quirky**
R	**raspberry**
S	**stone**
T	**talon**
U	**upper**
V	**variation**
W	**waste**
X	**xenophobe**
Y	**yammer**
Z	**zoom**

---

[2]You may want to photocopy the worksheets in this chapter so that you can use them more than once.

After you've completed your list, write at least three sentences that use words from your list **in sequence**. Use as many of the words in combinations as you can.

Example:

The **forlorn granola** looked lonely without milk and bananas.
"**Pale Quirky Raspberry**" was not a popular flavor at the ice cream shop.
I listened to that **xenophobe yammer** for an hour about illegal immigrants.

A
B
C
D
E
F
G
H
I
J
K
L
M
N
O
P
Q
R
S
T
U
V
W
X
Y
Z

SENTENCES:

1.

2.

3.

4.

5.

6.

On the worksheet provided, write at least three sentences following the format below:

WHO	**WHAT**	**WHERE**
The Mother Superior	dropped her rosary	on the steps of the Vatican.
The bus driver	yelled curses at the tourists	while waiting at the intersection.
The pizza delivery boy	stole a pound of mozzarella	on his way to basketball practice.

Now, switch the segments of your sentences around so that each of your Who's has a new What and Where:

1.   The Mother Superior yelled curses at the tourists on her way to basketball practice.

2.   The bus driver stole a pound of mozzarella on the steps of the Vatican.

3.   The pizza delivery boy dropped his rosary while waiting at the intersection.

Notice how each of these ordinary sentences becomes more interesting, creating an increased desire in the reader to know more about the characters.

Exercise No. 2 Worksheet

WHO	**WHAT**	**WHERE**
1.		
2.		
3.		

New sentences:

1.

2.

3.

<u>**Exercise No. 3 - Adjective Fire Drill**</u>   <u>**Time Limit: 15 minutes**</u>

On the worksheet provided, make a list of at least 10 simple adjective/noun combinations.

Example:

<u>**adjective**</u>	<u>**noun**</u>
rowdy	party
puffy	cloud
messy	room
sour	lemonade
melodramatic	actor
rainy	day
lively	music
warm	blanket
uncomfortable	shoes
silly	schoolgirl

Now, take the top adjective and move it to the bottom and move the rest up, leaving the nouns where they are. Notice how the new word combinations are much more interesting than the bland pairs in the first list.

Example:

puffy party
messy cloud
sour room
melodramatic lemonade
rainy actor
lively day
warm music
uncomfortable blanket
silly shoes
rowdy schoolgirl

Write at least three sentences using the new adjective/noun combinations.

Example:

The sour room had the atmosphere of a funeral parlor.
Her silly shoes were the center of attention and no one looked at her face.
The warm music loosened her up and gave her the urge to dance.

	adjective	**noun**
1.		
2.		
3.		
4.		
5.		
6.		
7.		
8.		
9.		
10.		

New List:

1.
2.
3.
4.
5.
6.
7.
8.
9.
10.

Sentences:

Chapter 3

GETTING STARTED

You can give fictional treatment to any of the NLP processes as a way of doing work on yourself or with someone else, creating a "metaphorical process" by telling or writing a story around it. It can be as simple as finding symbols for a present (or problem) state, resources and desired state. Most NLP processes boil down to these elements - getting from the present state to the desired state with the necessary resources.

It may be that you read a chapter on a particular process and come up with a brilliant idea for a story to work through it. If so, great. This will come so naturally to many of you that you'll wonder why you haven't been doing it all along. For others, the inner critic may have a particularly strong voice and may keep you from jumping in and writing your story. This chapter is for those folks who need a little jump-start in getting ideas for stories.

It's pretty simple: Follow each step of a process, allowing a symbol, metaphor, character, animal, or whatever to emerge and represent each element. These symbols do not have to "make sense" to the conscious mind, or have any obvious relationship to one another. Use each of the symbols or characters in your story, introducing them at the point that the step of the process would occur. This will also provide you with an effective vehicle for working content free. We can all get lost in content - our own or someone else's. By telling a story, you can really focus on the process - the content is irrelevant because you're dealing with it metaphorically

. For the purposes of this work, let's consider the difference between "elements" of the process and "steps" of the process. An *element* of the process might be: a problem state, a desired state, a resource, a future context (future pacing), a cue image, an unresourceful response, etc. You will be obtaining symbols or images for each element. *Steps* in the process might include: breaking state, anchoring, changing a submodality, establishing a dissociation. You will accomplish the steps of the process through your narrative and plot. Your story will be created around the movement of your hero from problem state to desired state. This will become clear when you read the chapters on how to give fictional treatment to the NLP processes.

When working on yourself, choose a time when you can relax and be free from interruptions, put on some soothing music and get comfortable. If you have a favorite meditation or relaxation visualization, this would be a great time to do it. Or, just take a few minutes to get in touch with your higher self, spirit guide, or whatever you choose to call your subconscious. If you are highly kinesthetic and you get a feeling about any of the elements in the process, just relax allow that feeling to become an image. Do the same thing if your first response is auditory - relax and allow that sound to become an image. This technique is used below to obtain a well-formed outcome. You will find similar worksheets at the back of the book for each of the six NLP processes covered in chapters 6 through 11. (You may want to photocopy the worksheets so that you can use them more than once.)

On rare occasions, you will work with someone who has extreme resistance to creating images. Sometimes you might just want to try something fun and different. In either case, use the following ideas to create symbols or metaphors for the steps in an NLP process. Mix and match from all 14 categories - using a different one for each step in a process. You'll be surprised at the delightful tales you can spin just by incorporating the objects, words and ideas that you come across every day.[3]

1.   Objects of all kinds - from ordinary stuff around the house to precious treasures and keepsakes.

2.   Pictures cut out of magazines.

3.   Photographs.

4.   Lines of poetry.

5.   Quotations.

6.   Song titles and lyrics.

7.   Book titles.

8.   Cartoons.

9.   Newspaper headlines.

10.   Fictional characters.

11.   Randomly selected words from the dictionary.

12.   Randomly selected pictures from books.

---

[3] I call this "Found Mythology;" see Chapter 13.

13. Historical, political or social figures - alive or dead.

14. Movie titles.

Ask the following questions and allow the images to appear; then, write or draw the symbol you receive for each question (I've left enough room for each symbol so you can draw, paste a picture, write a line of poetry, or whatever suits your purpose.) :

- **What do you want?**

Symbol:_____

- **When, where and with whom do you want it?**

Symbol:_____

- **How will you know when you have it?**

Symbol:_____

- **What resources, skills and abilities do you already have that will help you achieve your outcome?**

Symbol:_____

\-   What else do you need to achieve your outcome?

Symbol:_____

\-   What will change when you get your outcome?

Symbol:_____

\-   What is the first step you will take to get your outcome?

Symbol:_____

Some of the stories in this book are a result of actual issues that concern me and therefore contain symbols, imagery and themes that are relevant in my life: The nature of long term friendship, the division of resources, family dynamics, the loss of creativity and the transformation of the human heart.

I wrote other stories in the book using the various processes described above. Because they did not reflect any particular issue I was working on, I was able to concentrate on the process of doing NLP metaphorically; I found this to be extremely helpful and a lot of fun. When working with other people, I use the metaphorical process to obtain their symbols. Sometimes I offer them a story, and sometimes I have them write their own.

CHAPTER 4

USING NLP PRINCIPLES IN STORYTELLING

Ecology:

First, you need to have ecology with yourself around telling a story to someone, and thereby doing a metaphorical NLP process with them. Some stories come from deeper places within our soul than others, and you may not want to share it with someone else. Get congruent on this point, or you will be robbing yourself of a gift and the true meaning of your story will be largely lost on your audience. Once you are clear on this, you can proceed to share your stories with the world. (We'll discuss this further in Chapter 14.)

Next, you need ecology with your audience. Ask yourself:

- Why am I telling this story?
- Whose outcome do I have in mind?
- Will it enrich both the teller and the audience?
- Do I have permission to tell this story to my audience?

Rapport:

Permission comes from having rapport with your audience. You wouldn't attempt an NLP process on someone with whom you do not have rapport, and you'll follow the same guidelines for this type of storytelling.

This brings up another point: Do you have rapport with your characters? Do they have it with each other? How can this be a plot point in the story? Rapport, and the lack thereof, is cause for endless variations in human behavior and relationships. Use this principle to enrich your stories and give your characters real hearts and hands and eyes.

Presuppositions:

The NLP presuppositions[4] were developed to enrich our understanding of others' behavior. You could write volumes about the effect of operationalizing each of the presuppositions on systems large and small: relationships, families, communities, governments. When writing your

---

[4]See Chapter 16 for a list of the presuppositions rephrased especially for writers.

story, ask yourself the following questions:

– Am I applying the presuppositions to my characters' actions?

– How would my story be different if I did (or did not)?

– Are my characters applying the presuppositions to each other?

– How would my story be different if they did (or did not)?

– How can I operationalize the presuppositions in my narrative?

– What presuppositions am I applying to my hero?[5]

– What does this say about me? About my audience?

Representational Systems:

A good story includes sensory-based details for all the representational systems, which can be included in your narrative and your characters' dialogue. Ask yourself the following:

– Are the characters operating exclusively from a particular representational system? Am I?

– Is this a source of conflict in the story line?

– What would happen if a major shift occurred and their perceptual field opened up?

– How would you gracefully switch back and forth between representational systems in your narrative?

Perceptual Positions:

Whether you tell your story from first, second, third or fourth position will determine the "point of view" of your narrative. Please consider:

– What are the advantages of each position?

– How does each one limit you?

– How would you switch back and forth elegantly, without confusing your audience?

– What about your characters - which perceptual positions are they in?

– Are your characters stuck in one perceptual position?

– Is this a source of conflict in the story?

– How would a shift in perceptual positions change your characters' behavior?

---

[5]The word "hero," like doctor, philosopher or artist, is used here to describe persons of either sex.

Sensory Acuity:

You will use your own sensory acuity to gather the material to be a good storyteller; we'll discuss that more in Chapter 13. You should also use your sensory acuity to calibrate your audience (if you are telling your story out loud) to make sure that ecology and rapport are maintained. What about the sensory acuity of your characters? Ask yourself:

-   How would having more (or less) sensory acuity change the behavior of your characters?
-   Do they have a particular weak (or strong) area?
-   Is this a source of conflict in the story line?
-   How would a shift in sensory acuity affect your characters' behavior and the story?

Allow your audience to use their own sensory acuity and to have the experience of calibrating the difference between your hero's present state and desired state. You will want them to be able to see, feel and hear the difference after the transformation has taken place.

Information Gathering:

If you are designing your story for someone else, some artful information-gathering will assist you in getting a nice fit for that person. The more you know about their personal history and current issues, the more meaningful you can make the story for them. Consider the following as possible elements for exploration:

-   Important relationships
-   Peak experiences
-   Treasured keepsakes
-   Accomplishments

Well Formed Outcomes:

Consult the following model for information on how to incorporate the conditions necessary for well formed storytelling. Remember, it's only a guideline, so don't stick to it so fanatically that you wring all the creativity and spontaneity out of your storytelling. Use the model as a reminder that you have a responsibility to make sure that your story is consistent with your hero's outcome. Your audience will feel cheated if you pull a rabbit out of your hat for the sake of plot convenience.

If you take the time and care to weave the basic concepts of NLP into your storyline, it will increase rapport with your audience, and therefore increase the effectiveness of your "storywork."

A MODEL FOR THE WELL FORMED STORY

What does your hero want? (Desired State)
MOTIVATION
-Stated in the positive.
CONTINUITY
-Within their control.
-Based on their physical, mental, emotional and spiritual capacity in the context you have created.
-Appropriate "chunk size."
-Without huge leaps in logic or gaps in the plot.
THEME
-Meta Outcome.
-What are the over-arching statements about life?

How will he know when he has it?
EVIDENCE PROCEDURE
-How will you know when the story is over?
-What will your hero see, feel and hear when the story is over?
(Getting clear on this will keep you from ending your story too soon or letting it go too long.)

What else will change when your hero has his outcome?
ECOLOGY and CONSEQUENCES
-What does your hero stand to lose if they get their outcome?
-Who else will be affected?
-How will various systems be affected?
     -Relationships?
     -Families?
     -Communities?

When, where and with whom does he want it?
SETTING
-What is the environment? What is the time frame?
NARRATIVE
-Use sensory-based narrative and dialogue to "show and tell."
-What is the genre of your story?
CHARACTERS
-Who are the other people in your story?
-However outrageous, are they plausible, given the context?

What stops your hero from having his outcome now?
CONFLICT
-How are they stuck?
-How are they "invested" in the present state? What is the secondary gain?
-What are their self-imposed limitations?
-What are their environmental or physical limitations?

What resources does your hero already have?

What additional resources does your hero need?
SUBPLOTS
-Gifts?   -Personality traits?
-Other People?   -Material Possessions?
-Skills and Abilities?   -Talents and Resources?
-Lessons?   -Awareness?
-Time?   -Experience?

How will your hero get there?
PLOT
-What is your story line?
-What are the plot points?
-Is there more than one way to get there?
-What is the first step?
-Is it appropriate and achievable, given the context?
-What is a plausible, systemic sequence of events that leads your hero to his outcome?

CHAPTER 5

MILTON MODEL LANGUAGE

I placed this section apart from the chapters that follow because the Milton Model isn't an NLP process *per se*, but a way of using language to influence and facilitate change. It is used in most effective NLP processes, and therefore can be incorporated into any of your stories. Use of Milton Model language tends to produce a trance-like state, as does most good storytelling. Consider the start of most fairy tales: "Once upon a time...," which is an invitation to time travel. Anytime you ask your audience to stretch their awareness of time and space, you are inducing a light state of trance.

A balance is struck in good fiction between providing exciting, sensory-descriptive detail that ignites the reader's imagination, and artful use of deletions, distortions and generalizations to create universal appeal.

When we hear something in a story that we recognize, we identify with the hero - his struggles, lessons and triumphs, and we make the journey, too. When we hear a story that we don't immediately understand, we go on a search through our subconscious to find the story's relevance to us. Both situations pull us into the story and require that we participate on different levels.

Elegant use of the Milton Model in your storytelling will give you the opportunity to enchant your listeners and yourself. I encourage you to re-read some of your favorite stories from childhood (and beyond) and notice how often Milton-type language is used.

I do not provide any original stories in this chapter. Instead, for each language pattern I offer two examples of how to incorporate Milton Model language into your own stories: (A) one for narrative and (B) one for dialogue. Consider how using this vague, artful language can make your characters' dialogue more interesting and increase the impact of your narrative:

1. Mind Reading: Claiming to know the internal thoughts or feelings of another.

    (A) As Neva walked through the village, she deliberately met the gaze of each person she passed. She knew what they were all thinking - that she had stolen the golden bell.

    (B) Peter screamed at his father, "I saw you sneaking out of the house, and I knew that you didn't care about me!"

2. Lost Performative: Value judgments where the performer of the judgment is not identified.

    (A) It's important for you to pay close attention to my story. You never know what you might learn!

    (B) The elders looked sternly at Mickey. "It's good for the town when we all cooperate," said old Denn.

3. Cause-Effect: Implication or direct statement that one thing causes another.

    (A) Kelsie knew that if she was patient enough and didn't cause any turmoil, eventually things would go her way.

    (B) Casey clutched the book to his chest and yelled at the crowd, "If you come one step closer, I'll throw myself off the cliff!"

4. Complex Equivalence: Where things or their meanings are equated as synonymous.

    (A) Sally saw the dead snake on the door step and knew that a visitor would soon appear.

    (B) "So, you finally decided to show up," said Nell. "I guess you're on the team."

5. Presupposition: The linguistic equivalent of assumptions.

    (A) Ben knew that his sister had the time, the intelligence and the patience to figure out the puzzle.

    (B) "You already know how to get home," said the wizard, taking away Jerome's map.

6. Universal Quantifier: Absolute generalizations lacking a referential index.

    (A) Even in the darkest of times, Cory always kept his chin up.

    (B) "You're never on time and you're never dressed properly," said the Queen as she dismissed her ladies in waiting.

7. Modal Operator: Words that dictate what is possible or necessary.

    (A) Sally walked faster down the forest path because she had to reach the shore before the ships arrived.

    (B) "Surely you must have realized that your actions would have serious consequences," said the constable.

8. Nominalization: A process (verb) which has been changed to an event (noun).

    (A) All Skyler wanted was a place to be quiet and have some freedom.

(B) "The world was not created to provide you with comfort," scolded the headmistress.

9. Unspecified Verb: Process words which lack a complete description.

    (A) As Tom walked among the villagers, he hoped that he blended in with them and would not be noticed.

    (B) "Pull yourselves together!" yelled the teacher when the students stood still in fear.

10. Tag Question: A question added at the end of a statement to displace resistance.

    (A) Delta hoped to escape the confrontation that awaited her. But it's funny how life hands out the exact lesson that you wish most to avoid, isn't it?

    (B) Kellen's uncle laughed when he saw the mess Kellen was in. "You've really done it this time, haven't you?"

11. Lack of Referential Index: Deletes who is doing the acting.

    (A) Someone could imagine the worst case scenario and not even come close to knowing the seriousness of the situation.

    (B) "A body has to wonder what's going on in that brain of yours!" said Aunt Cece.

12. Comparative Deletion: Words that imply a comparison but lack the object with which the comparison is made.

    (A) Loren felt if there were any justice, her brother would return.

    (B) "If you have any regard, please let me come with you," Sam begged her.

13. Pace Current Experience: Statements about the listener's current, on-going sensory experience.

    (A) As you listen to my little tale of adventure, you can remember our own journey toward enlightenment.

    (B) Grandma watched Lilly's little hands work the loom and said, "As you weave the thread, think of all the time your hands have learned to do something new."

14. Double Bind: Statements or questions which engage one's attention on a consequence which presupposes something else.

    (A) While in the back of his mind, Sam knew that he could always go home and try again, he saw the possibilities for conflict and maintained that it was not the best course, but that he should continue on his journey.

(B) "You can either work off your debt as my servant, or you can work in the fields harvesting the grain," said the sheriff.

15. Conversational Postulate: A yes or no question to which the listener responds by actually doing what is implied.

(A) Could you imagine what the monster looked like when it rose out of the lake and roared at the children?

(B) "Will you please stop referring to me as 'Your Highness'," pleaded Alison.

16. Extended Quote: Chaining a series of context which tends to overload one's conscious attention and dissociate what is being said by the speaker.

(A) Carol's eyes closed when the teacher said she would tell a wonderful story that had been told to her by her grandfather; because Joan said the story wasn't interesting at all and she had already heard it last year.

(B) "If I've told you once, it's a million times already, how your Uncle Pete said to be careful on the docks because he was told by the captain of his ship to watch for the big waves," said Jill's mother.

17. Phonological Ambiguity: Homonyms (in **bold**) which create mild confusion.

(A) It looked as if Jeff had a lot of **training** to do before he could work for the railroad.

(B) "Everyone **hear** listen to me good!" shouted the traveling salesman.

18. Punctuational Ambiguity: Connecting two phrases with a "pivot" word (in **bold**) as the last word of the first phrase and the first word of the second phrase.

(A) Everyone was having a wonderful **time** to get back to the camp and build a fire for the night.

(B) "I've been here **before** I go I need to say good-bye," thought Elsie.

CHAPTER 6

CONFLICT INTEGRATION

Summary of the Process:

1. Access two extreme parts that are in conflict.
2. Elicit the outcome of each in positive terms.
3. Determine the advantages of each position.
4. Anchor the separation.
5. Obtain mutual appreciation of the positive outcomes and the advantages each side has that the other does not have, but needs.
6. Integrate the polarities, creating a balanced, unified whole, with elements that neither could produce alone.
7. Future pace.

Purpose of the Process:

This process can be used in any situation where there is internal conflict or ambivalence. It is used to sort out the opposing sides of a conflict, identify the positive intention and unique advantages of each side and then to blend them together.

Fictional Treatment:

I heard somewhere long ago that there are only three plots in all fiction: Man versus man (this was prior to political correctness), man versus nature, and man versus self. I don't know if this is true, but it does make the Conflict Integration process appear ripe for fictional treatment.

The conflict integration story begins with a whole, which may or may not already show signs of fissure. The separation of the two parts can be due to any one or a combination of:

– Circumstances.

– The passage of time.

– Trials and tribulations (wars, famines, natural disasters).

– Misunderstandings or missed communication.

– Forces of nature.

Consider some creative ways to imagine the two parts:

– Yin and Yang.

– Light and shadow.

- Good and evil.
- Past and future.
- Life and death.

Let the concept of opposites fuel your imagination, then develop the opposites into characters or objects that will drive your story forward with intensity.

To create tension in your plot, include a period of refusal of both parts to unite - an unwillingness to acknowledge the benefit of coming together. The two parts may also be unaware of each other, or unaware that they need each other.

The circumstances precipitating the integration will be the main focus of your plot. Your story may be an epic adventure that spans decades, or it may take place in an afternoon, but eventually each part must recognize the other's positive intent and complementary nature.

The story ends with the profound realization that the two opposites, once united, can create something that neither can create on their own, the sum being greater than its parts.

The two example stories I provide use living creatures as the characters, so there is some awareness on the part of each party as to what is missing and free will is exercised during the process of the integration, recognition of the unified whole, etc. I encourage you to experiment with this format using objects instead of characters for the conflicted parts. Here are some ideas to get you thinking about how to do this:

- Your hero finds one half of a stone tablet. The writing on it makes no sense without the other half.
- Your hero has a key that will open a missing lock and reveal the secrets of the universe.
- Your hero finds a map that shows the way to a sacred temple. The legend showing how the distance is measured and what the symbols mean has been torn off.
- Your hero receives a book of poems from a dying friend or relative. It is written in a language no one understands. Only one other person in the world can translate the writing.

Story lines for the above examples would center around your hero's discovery of the part, the recognition that it is not whole, and the adventure in finding the other half and reuniting the two.

PHOEBE & PHILOPENA

In a long ago land bordering a sea with a strange name that I can't remember and never could pronounce, lived two friends named Philopena and Phoebe. They had known each other since they were very small girls, had gone to school together, learned of love and pain together, shared victories and vices, secrets and ceremonies. Phoebe was tall and fair and had big, strong hands and a musical voice. Philopena was dark and quick with warm brown eyes and a determined chin.

As they grew to be young women, they began to discuss their futures: Would they stay in their village, learn trades from their elders, marry, have families and settle into the quiet, productive lives of their mothers? Or, would they breathe in the salt air of the sea, set forth on adventure and sail for the far horizons? They shared hours of discussion over food, around small campfires and on the banks of fishing streams.

Their studies completed, and on the very brink of womanhood, they pooled their resources and purchased a small, sturdy boat. They spent weeks patching, painting and polishing the craft, stocking supplies and studying maps. At last the day came when the two friends would set forth on their adventure into the unknown waters beyond their harbor home. When the sun was barely a glow on the horizon, they kissed, hugged and promised their way out of their families' arms. Waving and smiling, they slipped away toward the horizon and into their future, leaving behind proud fathers, worried mothers and envious little brothers.

For days they sailed the calm seas and talked of the exciting times that awaited them. What about strange new lands would they encounter, populated with exotic people whose customs and festivals and hats were different than their own? What of foreign men with accents who would seduce them with their charms? What of the tales they would have to share when they returned to their small village would make them heros in the eyes of women and goddesses in the eyes of men. They dreamed of bringing home treasures unimagined and stories of wondrous times.

Each night they took turns keeping watch for the dangers of the sea: strong and unpredictable currents, sudden changes in the weather, and rocks and reefs that could appear as quickly as a spring rain. Then one night Phoebe was certain it was her turn to sleep and that Philopena would keep watch. Philopena was just as sure that it was her turn to rest and that

Phoebe would keep a lookout for their safety. Both of them fell asleep, leaving no one to steer their boat and keep watch for danger in the dark night.

Sometime during the night, Philopena and Phoebe woke in time to race to the deck and feel their craft torn apart on small but prominent reef - one that was clearly marked on their map, had either of them been navigating. Cold water washed over both of them and they found themselves in the stormy sea, clinging to a piece of their splintered ship.

They glared at one another - each blaming her shipmate for the foul misfortune that had befallen them. Neither said a word as they both fell into dreams of shame, guilt, blame and anger. While they slept, their fragile raft split in two pieces and drifted apart - Philopena's half silently floating north while, unaware, the sleeping Phoebe drifted south.

Before dawn the next day, Phoebe washed ashore on a small island. Awakened by the grating of the boards against the sand, she blinked her eyes against the pain of the bright sunlight. A few hundred yards away, Philopena landed on another island. As she came ashore, her head made acquaintance with a small rock, and she awoke with a start, rubbing her temple.

Phoebe crawled ashore and looked at her new surroundings. The island was small, but lush with trees and plants. She noticed that there were plenty of papaya trees and a fresh water stream that fed into the ocean. Many of the tall trees had long vines that reached the ground. At least there is food, she told herself, and we can build a tent with these vines and some leaves. She looked around for Philopena.

Meanwhile, Philopena struggled to her feet and surveyed the island where she had washed ashore. The beach soon gave way to a dense forest full of tall, strong mango trees. Fruit and old branches lay on the ground. At least we can eat, she thought and have wood to build a fire. She heard running water and saw a small waterfall crashing over a rock and flowing to the sea. Philopena turned to tell Phoebe of her discoveries, only to find that Phoebe was not on the island with her.

Philopena began to walk the perimeter of her island and about halfway around she saw another island, not unlike the one upon which she found herself. She squinted against the glare of the sun and thought she saw a figure on the shore - Phoebe! Phoebe jumped up and down and waved at Philopena. Both women ran to the edge of the sea and looked across the water at one another.

The sea between the two small islands was rough and dark - choppy waves broke the surface and the slender shadows of sharks darted back and forth, waiting for a weak fish or a foolish person to make themselves available for lunch.

Phoebe yelled to Philopena, "Swim across the channel and join me on my island!."

"You swim across," shouted Philopena, " and join me here!" Both shook their heads from side to side, crossed their arms in determination and dug their heals in the sand. Both thought, "I will not swim across to join her - if she's so keen on me, she can swim over here and join ME!"

Night fell and Philopena dined on mangos and some raw mussels she had pulled from the rocks. She fashioned a lean-to from fallen mango trees. Phoebe ate a supper of papayas and some small fish she had plucked from a shallow tide pool. Both slept and dreamt of betrayal: "How could I spend my whole life being best friends with someone who won't swim a few yards to join me."

Days and nights multiplied, doubling and tripling into weeks. Phoebe and Philopena each arose, fished, gathered, and marked time on their respective islands until one day Mother Moon waxed to her fullness and the lowest of low tides occurred. There appeared between the two islands a small strip of land; a strip just wide enough for a woman to walk across.

Philopena raced to the edge of the sea and yelled to Phoebe, "Walk across and come to my island!"

"You walk across and come here!" shouted Philopena. Both were annoyed and hurt that their best friend, their confidant since childhood, would not take a few steps to come over and visit their island, so again both dug their heels in the sand and stared at one another until the big sun set its red and brilliant self, and Mother Moon sent her tide back into the channel and their chance to be together was gone.

For another month, Philopena and Phoebe arose and fished and gathered and walked their islands and drank clear water and watched the night skies and thought of home and each other and their families and each other and the harvest festival in their village and each other and what would become of them. And they slept and dreamt of treasures just beyond their reach - so close that their fingertips grazed diamonds, gold and pearls. And then they would awaken, the feeling of just-missed opportunities still fresh upon their skins.

In the fullness of time, with the new cycle of Mother Moon, the lowest of low tides came again and the choppy water in the channel slid away, and the sharks sought deeper cover and the small spit of land appeared again, joining the two islands. This time, it was a wiser and softer Phoebe that ran to the island's edge and a humbler and more thoughtful Philopena who raced to the lapping sea. This time, the two friends waved and smiled and each took one step onto the slender ribbon that connected their two worlds. This time, they kept taking steps, two, three, four and then those steps became leaps and the leaps became bounds and they were running towards each other, with salt tears in their eyes and salt sea on either side of them. They reached each other in the middle of the sand bar and clasped hands -hard- and held on, laughing and crying, not wanting to speak, but just to feel the presence of each other.

"Why didn't you come to see me?" asked Phoebe.

"Because I was afraid of the strong current and the high waves," said Philopena, "Why didn't you come see me?"

"Because I was afraid of the sharks," said Phoebe.

They embraced each other - all their judgments gone. Phoebe had also been afraid of the swift current and the waves that were as tall as she was. Philopena had also seen the silhouettes of the sharks under the water and had been frightened of their silent determination.

Finally understanding each others' fears, the rest of the trouble seemed to burn away like morning fog: Phoebe had stayed her island with only the singing frogs for company because she did not want to die in the sea and Philopena had lived alone on her island with only the chattering birds as her friends because she did not want to die in the sea. And they were both still alive - so they had done alright for themselves and for each other.

"Listen," said Phoebe, "I have papayas and clear, fresh water on my island, plus long, sturdy vines."

"And I, " said Philopena, " have mangos and lots of trees."

"With your trees and my vines, we can make a raft, " said Phoebe.

"And, with your papayas and my mangos and plenty of fresh water, we can make the journey home," said Philopena.

They quickly worked together to bring vines and fruit to Philopena's island before the tide came in again and they spent the night lashing together the sturdy trees, making a seaworthy raft. They stocked up on fruit and fresh water and set sail with the next outgoing tide. On their journey home, the two friends talked of their childhood - boys they had known and hated and loved, camping trips, pranks, games, dreams and plans. Together they would return home and together they would nurture the precious thing that neither could create alone - friendship; and the stories the two of them would tell to their proud fathers, worried mothers and envious little brothers.

Recap of Story:

Write down which plot elements, dialogue or characters you think fulfill each of these steps of the process (See Chapter 17 for the author's recap).

1. Access two extreme parts that are in conflict.

    _____

2. Elicit the outcome of each in positive terms.

    _____

3. Determine the advantages of each position.

    _____

4. Anchor the separation.

    _____

5. Obtain mutual appreciation of the positive outcomes and the advantages of each side.

    _____

6. Integrate the polarities, creating a balanced, unified whole.

    _____

7. Future pace.

    _____

A TALE OF TWO MONKEYS

Deep in the forest, next to a dreamy river there grew a huge banana tree. Each day it watched the morning mist snuggle up to the sky at dawn and then watched each night as the sun slid down like a big gold pocket watch being slipped back into a vest. The tree had been there long enough to see ten generations of crocodiles lay their eggs on the sandy banks, hatch out and swim into the river. And, as everyone knows, crocodiles live a very long time. Some of them still remember their great, great, grandparents' stories about their cousins the dinosaurs who lived in forest along with them. That was before the big rock came. Before the thousand year night.

This particular banana tree had broad, green shiny leaves, heavy bunches of bananas and a strong thick trunk. When the warm wind was just right, the sweet smell of those bananas drifted up the river like a silk cloud and made the honey bees so jealous that they flew in crazy circles. The tree was a home to the bats and the butterflies, with shade from the midday heat and shelter from the afternoon rains. The bats and butterflies got on quite well in the old tree, sharing branches, leaves and small hollows in the trunk.

The old tree, not having chosen where to take root and thrive, grew right at the edge of the river. And, its long branches reached to the other side of that very same river. So, as you can well imagine, with the trunk being on one side of the river, and the branches being on the other side of the river, it wasn't quite clear which side of the river actually owned that elegant old tree.

It might never have been a problem, for the river itself wished to make no issue of ownership and the wet, sandy soil in which the tree took root would never have dreamed of staking claim. Of course, the sky itself merely enjoyed the tickle of those shiny, green leaves and would never think of asking for title to the tree.

No problem should have been made of this great tree's existence on the planet, except for two tribes of monkeys: the bat eared monkeys who lived on the side of the river where the tree took root and grew; the ring tailed monkeys who lived on the side of the river where the branches bent down and touched the banks with their heavy fruit. And, oh, those monkeys, how they loved to taunt each other. Why, sometimes, when the moon was full and yellow, they would line up on the banks of the river and taunt each other just to hear their voices carried across the night sky. And what did those mindless monkeys fight about? Why, the bananas, of course. Those bananas, creamy and sweet, caused a mountain full of strife in the quiet forest.

The bat eared monkeys reasoned, with some logic to their credit, that the bananas belonged to them because the tree grew on their side of the river. And the ring tailed monkeys had it figured, and you can understand their point, that the bananas belonged to them because the branches of the tree touched on their side of the river.

This debate raged for many years. Not nearly as long as the crocodiles had been spying on the white cranes to see when they left their nests alone and full of unprotected eggs, but for many years just the same. There was a tedious carnival of arguing week after week, month after month, and in moments of great frustration, when emotions ran high and humid, the occasional rock or stick was thrown across the river.

One day, Shango, the leader of the bat eared monkeys, overheard two elephants talking. "We must build a new road before the rains come, so that we can cross the river safely," one said.

"Yes," the other replied, "but this banana tree will have to be uprooted and felled so that the road will be wide enough." With that, the two elephants went about their business of surveying the forest and planning paths, routes and byways, because the elephants are the engineers of the forest, you know. They walk about casually enough, looking as though they have nothing more in mind than to strip a pale, green tree of its juicy leaves or to wallow in a muddy bank to keep the flies off their skin. But, they are mindful of every step they take and its effect on the forest and its tenants. A clump of brush cleared, an old log moved off a path - all this the elephants did in service of shaping, nurturing and directing the growth of the forest so that all her creatures were served and the river ran clean and nothing was wasted. This had been their job for as long as their collective memory could recall. Not nearly as long as the crocodiles had flailed their big tails through the murky water in search of spawning toads to snack on, but a very long time just the same.

"This cannot be," thought Shango. "We cannot lose our banana tree. I will go quickly and tell Yorinda." Yorinda was the leader of the ring tailed monkeys. Normally, Shango would rather sit in rhinoceros dung at high noon during the season of the biting flies than have anything to do with her, but this was an emergency.

Shango crossed the river on a sturdy vine and sought Yorinda who, as you can well imagine, greeted him with a certain amount of scorn. "And what, pray tell, does the leader of the bat eared tribe want? Does he wish to yell at me with his shrill and silly voice about whose bananas I am feeding my children?" she asked.

"Please Yorinda, I beg of you to listen to me," said Shango and something in the set of his brow and the way he clutched his tail very tightly with both paws, got her attention. Yorinda leaned forward with her whole self and her eyes told him that she would listen.

"The elephants are planning to tear down the banana tree to build a new road before the spring rains," he said." "We must go together to their leader, Obojo, and tell him how important the tree is to our tribes. If we both go, he may listen and spare our tree."

Yorinda's response was immediate and sincere. "I agree," she said. And very soon, both of them set out on the journey through the forest to find Obojo, the wise old leader of the elephants. Obojo had lived many years in the forest, as long as anyone could remember. Not so long as the crocodiles had been sunning themselves on flat rocks and grinning at passing fish, but very long just the same.

After a night and most of the next day, they reached the home of the elephants where they were greeted by the somber faces of the same elephants that Shango had overheard in the forest casually discussing the demise of the banana tree. They asked, with great respect, if they could have an audience with Obojo. The two elephants silently stepped aside and as the two monkeys approached Obojo, he said to them, "What is this I see? The leader of the bat ears and the leader of the ring tails here in the same clearing. Yet I hear no yelling and taunting and I see no rocks flying through the air. How can this be?"

Yorinda and Shango both bowed their heads, embarrassed that their antics had reached the wise ears of Obojo and were now fodder for his famous scorn. Their embarrassment soon gave way to their desperation, however, and they began to plead with Obojo, each taking turns and finishing sentences and adding on where the other left off.

It went something like this: The fruit of the great banana trees feeds both our tribes and what falls to the ground feeds the mouse-deer and the caterpillar. It provides shade in the summer and shelter in the winter. Its branches make homes for the birds and the fruit bats. It gives so much and asks so little in return. And the roots of the tree reach deep into the earth, for it is very old. Not so old perhaps as the crocodiles who open their jaws wide so the tick birds can clean their teeth, but very old just the same.

Obojo was quiet for a moment and then said, "I would think you both would be glad to see that old tree gone. It has been a source of distrust and animosity between your tribes for many years. Now you can be rid of it and perhaps you can live in peace."

Shango and Yorinda both stared at the ground, unable to think of a reply, for they both knew that Obojo spoke the truth. "Of course," said Obojo, "if you could find a way to share the fruit and not squabble over it, maybe we could build our road a little farther to the east."

"Yes!" cried both monkeys in agreement. "We will harvest the bananas and divide them evenly," said Shango.

"Agreed," said Yorinda, "our tribe will pick the fruit that hangs heavy from the branches on our side of the river and the bat ears can pick the fruit that grows high over the trunk on their side of the river!"

Obojo looked at Shango. "And do you agree with this plan?"

The fervent and sincere nodding of Shango's head up and down to show Obojo how serious he was about entering the agreement almost made him dizzy enough to fall over.

"Very well then," said Obojo. "Go in peace and never again fight over what is not yours to begin with. The banana tree gets its life from the soil and the river and the sun, not a bunch of selfish monkeys. The fruit the tree gives to you is a gift from the earth - to be shared and not hoarded, so that no one goes hungry."

Once the monkeys were safely out of sight, the wise old Obojo winked at his two lieutenants and there seemed to be, if one looked closely, just the slightest grin wrapped around his tusks. The two winked back at him and turned to make their way once again through the dense trees and brush, watching closely and listening intently for any hint of imbalance in the great forest or her children.

Shango and Yorinda thanked Obojo and made their way towards home. Skipping, leaping, twirling and swinging on vines they traveled together through the forest. Neither could contain their excitement and looked forward to bearing the good news to their tribes.

Upon Shango and Yorinda's return, there was much celebration. Both tribes crossed the river and visited each other - taking turns being host and visitor. Hands were clasped, babies were groomed and bananas were shared. There hadn't been a celebration the likes of this one in the forest for a long, long time. Not so long as a wily crocodiles had been sidling up beside unsuspecting eels and snapping them up for lunch, but a long time just the same.

Recap of Story:

Write down which plot elements, dialogue or characters you think fulfill each of these steps of the process (See Chapter 17 for the author's recap).

1. Access two extreme parts that are in conflict.

_____

2. Elicit the outcome of each in positive terms.

_____

3. Determine the advantages of each position.

_____

4. Anchor the separation.

_____

5. Obtain mutual appreciation of the positive outcomes and the advantages of each side.

_____

6. Integrate the polarities, creating a balanced, unified whole.

_____

7. Future pace.

_____

CHAPTER 7

SIX STEP REFRAME

Summary of the Process:

1. Identify unwanted behavior - something you do, but don't want to do.
2. Establish communication with the part that generates the unwanted behavior.
3. Distinguish the behavior from the positive intention.
4. Access the "creative part" and generate alternative behaviors to satisfy the positive intention.
5. Check ecology - determine if there are any objecting parts and if so, address their positive intent, generate new alternatives, etc.
6. Future pace.

Purpose of the Process:

This process is used to establish communication with a part of you that is producing unwanted behavior, find out that part's positive intention, and establish communication with a creative part that can generate alternatives to the unwanted behavior.

Fictional Treatment:

This process starts with the hero doing something that he does not want to do; this makes for a good story, since a flawed hero is usually more interesting than a perfect one. Why might your hero be stuck in unwanted behavior patterns?

– Is it family history?

– Does he have a natural talent that he is using for negative purposes?

– Is he under a spell?

– Is he locked into a role that he has always performed without question?

– Is it a sense of duty?

– Is it servitude for some past debt?

The possibilities are endless, and since this element of the plot is quite close to the concept of destiny, it makes for great for storytelling. It chunks up the problem and makes it systemic, rather than individual.

The next step is to have the hero communicate with the part of him that is doing the unwanted behavior.

- Does he have a dream?
- Does a mysterious messenger appear to him?
- Does an animal or something else without the power of speech suddenly begin to converse with him?
- Does he get a message in a bottle?

You could take a more down to earth approach and have the hero come to sudden awareness of this part and communicate with it internally.

Spend some time thinking about what form or shape this revelation would take for your hero:

- What would make sense?
- What would be meaningful?
- What would be symbolic of this part and its behavior?

It is important to lay the proper groundwork so that the next step - distinguishing behavior from positive intent - can flow naturally and not sound contrived. You're building a fictional universe here, but it still has to contain a certain logic. Just as you would when working with a client, ask the kinds of questions that would lead you to uncover the positive intent of this part: what is this part trying to do for your hero?

Now that your hero has come to awareness, he is on the road to resolution - getting in touch with the creative part that can generate alternatives for new behavior. The tendency here might be to bring in a fairy godmother, genie in a bottle, or magic wand to do the trick, which is exactly what this type of intervention would be - a trick.

When writing your stories, make the creative part a facet of your hero, either physical, emotional, spiritual or mental. Your story will be much more empowering if the creative part comes from within and not from some external source. Consider the following alternatives for expression of your hero's creative part.

- Higher consciousness.
- Spirit guide.
- Divination tool - runes, tarot cards, tea leaves.
- Meditation, prayer, fasting or other spiritual practice.

- Vision quest.

- Dream.

Now that the creative part has been contacted, it can get in touch with the part that is doing the unwanted behavior. They form an alliance to generate alternative behaviors to satisfy the positive intent of both. The richer a portrait you can paint of this bond, this pact, the more solid your story will feel. Work to build that relationship so that your audience gets the idea that, even after the story is told, this process continues and the work is still being done.

My favorite books have been ones that, after I had finished them and put them back on the shelf, made me feel as though the characters continued on with their lives while I wasn't looking. This is what you want to convey to your audience.

Before you can end your tale, you need to check for ecology. There may be other "parts" (whatever form they may take) that object to the change in behavior of your hero. This is the time for all to speak or forever hold their peace. Look around the landscape of your fictional universe and ask yourself: who else will this affect? Don't leave any loose threads hanging - this will diminish the power of your story and leave your audience with a vague feeling of unease.

You created these characters; they are your responsibility. You have an obligation to address how they might be affected by the change and to make sure that their objections are dealt with and satisfied.

Resist the urge to tidy things up with a "they lived happily ever after" ending. Think about the system or environment in which your hero lives and what it would take to satisfy each element so that everyone and everything can be aligned with the change in behavior.

Once you've dealt with any objections, it's time to future pace. This is where you have a great opportunity to give your audience a glimpse of how things will be different after the story has ended. Send your hero forth with all sorts of new options and alternatives.

- What might happen to him down the road?

- What adventures might he have?

- What fascinating characters will he meet?

Leave your audience with the notion that positive things will continue to evolve for this hero.

AFTER HOURS AT MRS. BLAYLOCK'S TOY STORE

Bubble Machine was going wild again. Every night, after old Mrs. Blaylock would sweep up and put the lights out, Bubble Machine would spin its handle and send the glossy orbs floating around the store. The other toys would scold, yell, plead, beg, bribe and cajole him to stop, but it was no use. The bubbles would float and then pop on whatever got in their way, leaving little splatters of soap all over the store.

It was quite distracting and interfered with a good night's rest. Sometimes, the bubbles fell on the floor and made slick spots; Rubber Duck would slip and slide on her belly and bump her bill into the wall. Sometimes, they would land on Scooter Car's windshield and he would drive around in circles, unable to see where he was going. Sometimes, they would fall on Nurse Doll's starched, white apron and make her look sloppy. No one could get Bubble Machine to open up and tell them what was going on. He just spun his handle and sent the bubbles forth in a steady stream each night. And, because Mrs. Blaylock filled his soap tank regularly, he always had a fresh supply.

One night, Sock Monkey decided enough was enough and he wiggled off his shelf and went over to Bubble Machine. He patted him with his soft, plushy paw and just sat there, waiting for him to let him know what was up. Soon, Bubble Machine slowed the spinning of its handle and told Sock Monkey he spun bubbles all night because he wanted to be King of the Toys. Sock Monkey giggled and told Bubble Machine that the honor of being King (or Queen) of the Toys didn't necessarily go to the toy that worked the longest hours.

Bubble Machine was confused and asked Sock Monkey to tell him how to be King of the Toys if it wasn't by working as hard as he could spinning bubbles day and night. Sock Monkey gently told Bubble Machine that the toy that gave the children the most joy, the one that they remembered most fondly and kept up on a shelf long after they stopped playing with it, the one that they would never dream of giving away no matter how old they got, that was the toy that got to be King or Queen.

Bubble Machine pondered this all night long and, instead of endlessly spinning bubbles into the air, he thought very hard about how he could be the very best toy at Mrs. Blaylock's. Meanwhile, the other toys finally got a good night's rest and it seemed there would be peace in the toy store at last.

While the other toys slept, Bubble Machine asked his soap tank, his handle, his bubble holes, his stand and the bright shapes painted on his front if they would all help him be the best toy in the store. At once they all agreed, except for the handle, who was a little afraid that he wouldn't have enough to do if they weren't making bubbles all night into the wee hours. Bubble Machine assured him that if they all worked harder to make children happy, more children would want to play with him and that the handle would have plenty to do. The handle was happy and agreed to help out.

The next day, Mrs. Blaylock opened the store and stopped to look around after she turned on the light. Something was different, but she couldn't quite put her finger on it. The toys looked the same as when she left them the night before, but they seemed...calmer. She chuckled to herself, "An old woman's imagination!" As she turned to unlock the cash register, she didn't see Sock Monkey wink his button eye at Bubble Machine.

Recap of Story:

Write down which plot elements, dialogue or characters you think fulfill each of these steps of the process (See Chapter 17 for the author's recap).

1. Identify unwanted behavior.

_____

2. Establish communication with the part that generates the unwanted behavior.

_____

3. Distinguish the behavior from the positive intention.

_____

4. Access "creative part" and generate alternative behaviors to satisfy the positive intention.

_____

5. Check ecology - determine if there are any objecting parts and if so, address their positive intent, generate new alternatives, etc.

_____

6. Future pace.

_____

SELF REFLECTION

He carried one in his pocket. There was a big one inside his front door - in the hallway. He had two in his office. Luckily, his car came equipped with two - one on the driver's side and one on the passenger side. Then, of course, there were the store windows, rain puddles and car windshields. All the world, it seemed, provided him with mirrors. To check his hair, his tie, his expression.

He often wondered about his compulsive need to verify his looks in a reflective surface, but life seemed to be going too fast for him to really delve into the reasons. He rationalized that he had to look good for business, and he wanted to look good for personal reasons - so what was the big deal? He had the nagging feeling that he was compensating...looking at his reflection and not at himself. Accepting a two-dimensional substitute for the real thing. He didn't look inward, but he sure had a handle on whether his tie matched his shirt.

He reasoned with himself from time to time that life was competitive and he had to make a good appearance. He was just keeping up with the pack, he would think to himself, and if he was lucky, he'd stay a little bit ahead. "But..." asked a voice, small and distant, "was there more? Was there a better way? Was there something missing?"

When he was younger, he trusted his brains, his intuition, and his verbal agility to get him places. When did he stop relying on those aspects of himself and begin to depend on expensive suits and manicures? He knew that, somewhere along the line, he had sold himself out, and he wondered if he could get back the edge that had once come so naturally...without a cell phone and a late model car.

What if the other executives get vacation homes? Sailing yachts? Trophy wives? He would compete with his talent, his smarts and his energy, like the old days. Like he used to, when he was hungry and the world was his picnic.

Italian leather and state of the art electronics had nothing on the pure rush of adrenaline that came with the drive to be number one. When all burners were ignited, it came down to the still, small point of energy that pushed him forward and kept him going. Like a laser beam, it cut through the superfluous trappings of "the good life" and kept him focused on the goal. It shined so brightly he could see himself and, you know, he didn't look half bad.

Recap of Story:

Write down which plot elements, dialogue or characters you think fulfill each of these steps of the process (See Chapter 17 for the author's recap).

1.   Identify unwanted behavior.

_____

2.   Establish communication with the part that generates the unwanted behavior.

_____

3.   Distinguish the behavior from the positive intention.

_____

4.   Access "creative part" and generate alternative behaviors to satisfy the positive intention.

_____

5.   Check ecology - determine if there are any objecting parts and if so, address their positive intent, generate new alternatives, etc.

_____

6.   Future pace.

_____

CHAPTER 8

VISUAL SWISH

Summary of the Process:

1. Find a cue image that is seen just before an unwanted behavior or reaction.
2. Break state.
3. Using positive submodalities, create a desired state image or "wonderful self" image.
4. Shrink the desired state image of the wonderful you down to the size of a dot. Place the dot containing the desired state image in the center of the cue image. Imagine the cue image getting smaller and darker while, simultaneously, the dot image of the desired state or wonderful self image gets larger and overwhelms the cue image.
5. Repeat step 4.
6. Test and future pace.

Purpose of the Process:

The visual swish is used when someone has an adverse response to a visual cue. Such responses can include, worry, stage fright, performance anxiety, jealousy and anger. The process can also be used to eliminate compulsive consumption of certain foods and assist with smoking cessation and obsessive/compulsive disorders.

Fictional Treatment:

A story containing a swish process will most likely be one of action or force of nature. There must be some swift movement in order to attain the appropriate intensity of growing the desired state image from something tiny to something big enough to overcome the cue image or present state.

You'll start by establishing the cue image, and here you have a lot of latitude. Think about what would make for an interesting "stuck state" for your hero:

– What unresourceful reaction do they have to a stimulus in their life?

– What habits or compulsions are detracting from the quality of their life?

This is the first process we've worked with wherein you must establish a "break state," so play with this one and have some fun. How can you metaphorically create a break state or a neutral state?

– Sleep.

- Darkness.
- Fog.
- Rain.
- Clouds.
- Murky water.
- A curtain.
- Looking through a glass darkly.
- Amnesia.
- Bright light.

In the swish process, the break state is used to distinguish between present state and desired state. Once you establish the context of your story, think about what might occur naturally that would create a "break state" for your character, what they might encounter in their universe that would sufficiently neutralize an upsetting cue image.

The swish process calls for establishing a "wonderful self" that has already handled the problem state. I encourage you to experiment with this. Those purists among you may find a way to incorporate this step into your stories. If you find it to be cumbersome, swish from a problem state to a desired state and then integrate the "wonderful self" aspects into your hero's character after the desired state had been achieved.

You must establish a desired state and - here's the tricky part - be able to make it very small. What are some circumstances that make large things seem small?
- The passage of time.
- The perspective of long distance.
- Being seen out of a small opening.
- Shrinking with exposure to sun or water.
- Fading with loss of memory.
- Breaking something into small pieces.
- Folding something like paper or cloth.
- Stuffing something into a small container.
- Obscuring by dirt, dust, mud, etc.

Again, the context of your story will determine what makes sense. Remember, you must make the desired state big again, so take this into account. This can be accomplished for all of the above examples by reversing the process that lead to the shrinking in the first place. For example, if something dries up in the sun and shrinks, you can add water to make it large again. If it is folded, like a piece of paper, it unfolds back to its original size, etc.

Look to the four elements of nature for assistance in this process. All four - wind, fire, earth and water - have mystical and practical transformative powers. Wind erodes and cleanses the landscape; fire sterilizes and chemically alters almost all substances exposed to it; the earth can hold a seed until it sprouts and becomes a huge tree; and water can cleanse and refresh. And all carry enough force to power your "swish" process.

Think about the four elements, and other forces of nature, and what forms they might take in your story line:

- How might your characters cleverly use the gifts of nature to help them transform themselves?

- What alliances can they form with other species - a horse, a dolphin, a hawk, a cheetah - that would give them the appropriate power and speed?

The instructions of the swish process indicate that it should be repeated at least three times with increasing speed, or as many times as necessary to achieve the desired results. Because you are dealing with fictional characters here, this has to be a judgment call on your part and will largely depend on the context of your story. I would, however, encourage at least one repetition to reinforce the transformation for your audience.

Although not essential for success, future pacing is always a nice touch in an NLP process. To stretch yourself as a storyteller, consider ways in which you can future pace your characters. Think about some unique ways in which you might accomplish this:

- Time travel.
- Fortune telling.
- Dreaming.
- Encountering the situation again in the story.
- Telling your story in flashback.

Let your audience know that the transformation was successful by having your hero encounter the original cue image and responding resourcefully.

MAX'S WALL

When Max first came to the home, he was able to move around. He could still hold a paint brush, feed himself and do those other things he had taken for granted all those years. But, the years passed and his body fell under the spell of time and gravity, leaving Max in a wheelchair. He had to be rolled about - pushed from behind - which was the thing he hated the most. Not able to see who was behind him pushing him forward, wheels squeaking on the worn linoleum. Pushed up to the window to spend hours watching nothing. Looking at the old wall in the east garden.

Max used to spend a lot of his time in the garden. He brought all his paints and brushes with him and got permission from the chief of staff to paint the wall. He started at one end and slowly worked his way along and painted all the things he had enjoyed in his life. A trip to Coney Island. Coming home from the war. His wedding day. His first new car. He painted memories on that wall, one by one, until the wall was filled with the moments from Max's life, moments that stand out as you look back over eighty or so years.

He had been a sign painter and painted pictures on things laying around the house, garage and garden, any surface that was still long enough. His wife used to tease that he would have painted the kids if they hadn't been so fast. He had outlived his wife and both sons. It is a terrible thing to outlive your kids. It goes against all the laws of nature.

On his eightieth birthday, Max was told by his doctor that he had a disease that would eventually rob him of his breath, so he sold everything and moved out here to this home near the edge of the desert. The air was dry and the weather was warm. That's what his doctor said he needed for his lungs. The warm, dry air did help his breathing but didn't keep the forces of time from eventually taking away the use of his legs and hands.

He didn't miss walking as much as he missed his painting. He kept a few old jars of paint in his room and would ask the attendants to open them once in a while, just so he could smell them. He could remember when he was their master and the colors blended and the brushes moved at his will. The staff thought it was an odd but harmless request, so obliged him when they were not too busy with other things.

Max sat at the window on this dry day and looked out at the wall he had painted some five years ago - or was it six? It was now caked with sand and mud and leaves and whatever else had blown by and gotten stuck there. All that he could see of his paintings was one small corner - the bright colors of a beach ball. That was from the time he and his wife had first taken their little boys to the ocean. They had spent a whole week - swimming, playing, eating salt water taffy. The boys had loved it and so had Max.

He would look at the corner of the wall and the bright blue, green, red, yellow of the beach ball his little boys had played with on the shore. Soon that would be covered too, he thought, and there would be nothing of his wall left. Max hoped he would die first. He hated seeing his wall all covered up and caked with mud and dirt. He felt like he was caked with mud and dirt as well, that he was covered with years worth of debris like his wall and that he had lost his color, too.

And then Max would nod a few times and his chin would rest on his chest. He would sleep right there in his chair until one of the attendants came and wheeled him back to his bed, or into the television room where he joined others like himself who slept in chairs during the day.

One morning the anonymous voice behind him commented as he pushed Max to the window that it looked like a rare desert storm was off in the distance. Max saw the black clouds gathering on the horizon and wondered if he could stay awake long enough to see the storm. It would at least be something different, something to remind him that a wild and powerful force still existed in the world. Something to listen to other than his wheelchair squeaking on the linoleum and the shuffling of old, slippered feet.

The wheelchair stopped in front of the window, the voice said goodbye to Max and he was left alone to look at his wall again. He eyes went to the place where his beach ball was still visible and for a terrible minute, Max could not find it. A tumbleweed blew away, exposing bright colors again. Max was so relieved he almost began to cry and then felt ashamed that a square foot of wall with some bright paint had come to mean so much to him.

Max's ears were still sharp and he could hear the storm approaching. Max looked out to the horizon again and saw the black clouds getting closer. He thought he could hear rumbling, too. Yes, it was thunder. If he could spot a flash of lightening and then count - one Mississippi, two Mississippi, until he heard the thunder again, he could tell how many miles the storm had to travel.

At least that was what he father had taught him to do, as he had taught his boys. Neither of his own sons had any children to teach. One was lost in Viet Nam, just nineteen years old, the other died in a house fire six years later. Then Max did what he usually did when his memories traveled to painful territory: he nodded a couple of times and let his chin drop, and sleep, that wonderful angel, came and gave Max a rest from his loneliness.

Max awoke to a loud clap and the rattle of the windows. His head snapped up and he was alarmed and delighted to see that the thick, dark clouds, once on the distant horizon, were now surrounding the home. The sky outside had a purplish cast to it and the hairs on Max's arms stood up from the electricity in the air. Max was still taking all of this in when the first huge, wet drop of rain slapped against the window, then another, and soon the window had sheets of water pouring down it.

Max was more excited than he had been in years because through the thick rain and the purple air, he could see something amazing. The wind was driving the rain across Max's wall with such force that, in a matter of seconds, years of mud, sand and old dried leaves were washed away and the wall was clean again.

For a moment, Max thought he had imagined it in an old man's excitement about a summer storm, so he replayed it in his mind. First he could just see the corner with his bright beach ball and then, the rain and wind teamed up and washed the length of the wall clean. Max rubbed his eyes and looked again. There again were the scenes from his life - his family, his accomplishments, the good memories, memories he held dear and could now see again in big, bright colors.

Max sat and watched the storm die down. The rain slowed until he could hear the individual drops on the window again, and then stopped altogether. The black and purple clouds blew over the home on their way to give someone else in the desert the gift of a storm. The sun came out and the colors on Max's wall so much were brighter than he remembered. They were gift, a promise and a miracle after the fury of nature, a rainbow of Max's memories.

Recap of Story:

Write down which plot elements, dialogue or characters you think fulfill each of these steps of the process (See Chapter 17 for the author's recap).

1. Find a cue image that is seen just before an unwanted behavior or reaction.

   _____

2. Break state.

   _____

3. Using positive submodalities, create a desired state image or "wonderful self" image.

   _____

4. Shrink the desired state image of the wonderful you down to the size of a dot. Place the dot containing the desired state image or wonderful you on the center of the cue image. Imagine the cue image getting smaller and darker while, simultaneously, the dot image of the wonderful you gets larger and overwhelms the cue image.

   _____

5. Repeat step 4.

   _____

6. Test and future pace .

   _____

KEEPSAKE

She heard him tinkering in the kitchen. It was that time again. She couldn't write - she couldn't even think - when he was in their making that god awful stuff. His special pickled garlic recipe, smelling like brine and ammonia, had come to annoy her more each year he made it for the Labor Day picnic. She had to get away from that stench.

She stomped past the kitchen on her way to the attic. She would go up and poke through boxes, straighten things out, knock down cobwebs. It was her way of escaping when he got on her nerves, which seemed to be a lot lately. He called out as she passed the kitchen door, "Hey, where you going? I'm just starting the garlic."

"I'm going upstairs to the attic so I won't have to smell that stuff," she said.

"You used to help me," he said. "You used to peel the garlic cloves for me."

"I used to wear bell bottoms, too," she said as she climbed the attic stairs.

She plopped down in front of a promising box full of old stuff. She could still smell the brine and hear him rattling around downstairs and it irritated her greatly. She settled in and raised a cloud of dust that made her sneeze.

She removed the first thing on the box. An old picture frame. She started to set it aside in a pile of things that could go to a garage sale, but noticed it contained a picture. All but the very edge of the left hand corner was covered in a thick layer of dust. She used the back of her hand to wipe the dust away and was amazed to find their wedding picture. It was taken as they ran for the car, holding hands, all smiles and opportunity, optimism and potential. So long ago.

The dust she had cleared from the picture frame made her sneeze again. She held still waiting for another one which didn't come. When she finally inhaled, she smelled that damn brine. This time, though, the irritation was lost in a flurry of white silk, birdseed and good wishes. She got up to go back to the kitchen to peel garlic cloves.

Recap of Story:

Write down which plot elements, dialogue or characters you think fulfill each of these steps of the process (See Chapter 17 for the author's recap).

1. Find a cue image that is seen just before an unwanted behavior or reaction.

   _____

2. Break state.

   _____

3. Using positive submodalities, create a desired state image or "wonderful self" image.

   _____

4. Shrink the desired state image of the wonderful you down to the size of a dot. Place the dot containing the desired state image or wonderful you on the center of the cue image. Imagine the cue image getting smaller and darker while, simultaneously, the dot image of the wonderful you gets larger and overwhelms the cue image.

   _____

5. Repeat step 4.

   _____

6. Test and future pace.

   _____

CHAPTER 9

CHANGE PERSONAL HISTORY

Summary of the Process:

1. Identify and anchor problem state (a troubling experience from the past).
2. Identify and anchor a resource (one that would have made it possible for you to have had a more productive, positive experience in the past situation).
3. Integrate by taking the resource state back into the problem memory and relive that experience in a new way.
4. Test and future pace.

Purpose of the Process:

This process is used to neutralize a memory of a past event that still evokes an unresourceful or negative reaction.

Fictional Treatment:

In a "change personal history" story, you can give your hero the opportunity to go back to the past with new resources and "re-live" the troubling event, thereby changing the present state of their life.

You can start your story by establishing some troubling experience from your hero's past - a memory that is somehow affecting the quality of his life in the present. The reminder of this event can take various forms, such as memory, a recurring dream or just the every-day self-recrimination that takes place when people think they've made a horrible mistake for which there is no clemency.

Consider some of the ways in which a perceived past mistake or missed opportunity affect the quality of peoples' present life:

- Can't let go - replaying the memory obsessively.
- Feelings of guilt, remorse and shame.
- Sabotaging relationships.
- Low self-esteem.
- Not reaching goals.
- Not taking care of your physical body.

These may seem like pretty mundane things to build a story around, but they are the stuff of human suffering — a theme that everyone can identify with on some level.

This is another story in which you need to establish a "break state." We discussed this at some length in Chapter 8. Consider the possibility that your hero's environment could be a way to break state: your hero could be thinking about the trigger event in the past - letting her mind wander, so to speak - when the daily demands of her current situation snaps her back to reality and is temporarily pushing the memory aside.

The actual process calls for an anchor of the problem state. Consider some of the ways you might "anchor" your audience to your hero's problem state. What does your hero see, feel or hear that provokes the memory? If described in sensory-based language, and used consistently throughout your story, this will be an anchor for your audience as well.

Next, your hero needs a resource that would have made a difference in the past event. This can make your story especially poignant. Who among us hasn't wanted to go back and do something differently? How often have you heard the phrase, "If I knew then what I know now..." With NLP, we **can** know then what we know now. Make the resource as specific and appropriate to the situation as possible.

I would also encourage you to make a point of honoring the presuppositions around the person's past behavior. Reframing the past "mistake" with: "There is no failure only feedback," or "People make the best choices available at the time," will alleviate the shame and self-recrimination with which your audience will identify.

The resource state also calls for an anchor. Consider ways your hero might be using the resource in the present or in another context. What do they see, feel or hear when the resource is evident? Anchor your audience to it by having some consistent element in place when the resource is being used.

In the process itself, you fire both anchors and integrate the resource into the past situation. By including in your narrative or characters' dialogue both of the anchors you established previously -- one for the troubling memory and one for the resource -- you can bring your audience to the setting where the integration can occur.

Now that your hero is ready to integrate, how might you create a situation for your hero to take his resource into the past and re-live that experience in a new way?

- Have him repeat an experience **very** similar to the previous one, using the resource. This would be especially meaningful if your hero has been avoiding such situations due to his past experience.

- Employ a "Christmas Carol" technique, where the hero is transported back in time and allowed to see, feel and hear himself re-living the event with the new resource.

- Have your hero's dreams, fantasies and imagination become venues for re-living a past event with a new resource.

To assure your audience that the transformation is real, test your hero by exposing him to the troubling memory again. This is where having established an anchor to the problem state will be helpful. The test will have credibility for your audience, because you've laid this groundwork for them. Now you have the opportunity to show and tell how different your hero's life is now that he has incorporated the resource into the memory.

As before, future pacing isn't absolutely necessary but will solidify the transformation for your audience. Let your imagination take you past the end of the story a little and give your audience a glimpse of what your hero's future will be like.

THE SILENCE OF THE SEA

Melanie couldn't believe what she heard in town and was on her way to see for herself if it was true. A couple from the city had bought the old lighthouse and they were moving in. What kind of people could live in such a place? As she approached the white tower, she stopped, barely catching her breath. Even after all these years, it made her throat ache to see it. She had planned to rush right up and question the new owners, but now she just turned her car around and drove back toward town.

She went out of her way not to drive or walk past the lighthouse. It was still too painful. If only she'd had more courage, if she'd been stronger, she could have stopped the arguing that led to the fighting that led to a shove and the two grappling bodies that fell to the rocks below. High school graduation had been somber that year. Two empty seats with black ribbons on them for the two boys who had lost their lives on the rocky shore beneath the lighthouse. Melanie still heard their screams in her sleep; they sounded not so much terrified as surprised. Utterly shocked at the prospect of their mortality. Then, nothing. Silence.

She had stood there and watched the argument escalate, gritting her teeth and thinking, "Go along to get along. Don't make waves - people might not like you." It was like that whenever she was around people she considered to be her social superiors. She had considered herself lucky to have been invited to the party that night, so she stood in silence while two young men in the prime of their lives wrestled each other off the lighthouse balcony.

Melanie went back to work at the child care center she owned. With the children and their parents, she was strong and confident. She handled problems easily and people sought her advice. The children loved and respected her and their parents dropped them off each day with the absolute confidence that they were happy and well cared for. She had often wished she could be the same way around other people as she was with the kids and their families. At work, she held her head up and looked right at people.

When Melanie arrived back at the center, the children were in the play yard. She started to go back into her office and finish some paperwork when a ruckus in the corner of the yard got her attention. One little boy, a red headed chap with a quick wit and a temper to match, had another boy by the hair and was holding on with both hands and demanding the return of a yo-yo. The other boy was kicking and swinging furiously, desperately trying to find some purchase on his enemy.

Melanie walked across the yard and laid her hands on the boys' shoulders and looked at them. Her purposeful expression and the pressure of her hands were enough to get their attention. She took each boy by the hand and led them back to her office where they discussed, with great civility, why their behavior had not been appropriate. She made them shake hands like gentlemen and sent them on their way.

She sat at her desk smiling at the successful resolution to the play yard dust-up. She leaned back in her chair and let her mind drift to that night in the lighthouse. This time, she saw it happening differently. She walked up to the two teenagers and laid her hands on each of them, firmly and calmly, something about her expression, her posture and the pressure of her hands got the boys' attention, and they stopped fighting long enough for common sense to prevail and the party to resume.

Melanie jumped when one of her assistants came in and told her the parents had started to arrive to pick up the children. She went out to the yard, waved and said good-bye, but she felt like she was moving slowly, as if through water and her voice sounded far away.

After work, she drove out to the lighthouse again. There was a big yellow moving van unloading boxes. "Good," she thought, "that old place has been empty too long." Melanie drove on by and waved to the new owners, a nice looking young couple. Artists maybe. Melanie decided she would let them get settled and then come out and introduce herself.

Recap of Story:

Write down which plot elements, dialogue or characters you think fulfill each of these steps of the process (See Chapter 17 for the author's recap).

1. Identify and anchor a problem state (a troubling experience from the past).

    _____

2. Identify and anchor a resource (one that would have made it possible for you to have had a more productive, positive experience in the past situation).

    _____

3. Integrate by taking the resource state back into the problem memory and relive that experience in a new way.

    _____

4. Test and future pace.

    _____

COOL SHADE

Peter sat down on the stone bench in the cathedral garden. It was hot and muggy and he was miserable. A few minutes of rest in the cool shade would do him good. He had just come from another painful client meeting. His need to defend, explain and justify had made a bad situation worse. "Why can't I just keep my mouth shut," he thought.

He glanced up at the ornate wall. On one end was a figure that captured his attention. It was a gargoyle with a huge, gaping maw; on either side of him sat little gremlins each pulling on the side of his mouth to stretch it even bigger. "That's me," thought Peter. "It's not as if my mouth weren't big enough already. I've got to go and stretch it even further to get myself in trouble."

He let his eyes wander across the wall to the other side. It was overgrown with ivy, thick and green. Another figure sat on the opposite corner. This one was a frog sitting lotus style. He wore a robe and had his arms folded and his hands tucked up inside his sleeves. He had a look of calm repose, almost smiling, infinitely patient. Peter imagined him sitting on a lily pad, Buddha like, waiting for a fly to come within striking distance.

Peter looked back over the ivy again at his likeness, the jabbering gargoyle, and thought how different things would be if he had the cool, inscrutable demeanor of the wise frog instead of the compulsive need to blurt out his every thought. He suddenly had an image of himself in that client meeting: sitting in his chair with his arms crossed and the stone frog's patient countenance.

He sat back and closed his eyes and imagined himself at that meeting or the next time trouble erupted at the office or a family tiff broke out; he thought of how it would be if he just sat, arms crossed, and listened to what was going on, saying nothing.

Peter smiled, slightly inscrutably, and thought that it seemed cooler already.

Recap of Story:

Write down which plot elements, dialogue or characters you think fulfill each of these steps of the process (See Chapter 17 for the author's recap).

1.   Identify and anchor a problem state (a troubling experience from the past).

_____

2.   Identify and anchor a resource (one that would have made it possible for you to have had a more productive, positive experience in the past situation).

_____

3.   Integrate by taking the resource state back into the problem memory and relive that experience in a new way.

_____

4.   Test and future pace.

_____

CHAPTER 10

MAPPING ACROSS SUBMODALITIES

Summary of the Process:

1.   Identify a problem state.
2.   Identify an appropriate resource state.
3.   Identify the differences between the visual, auditory and kinesthetic submodalities of each state.
4.   Map across by keeping the same content and changing the modalities one at a time.
5.   Test and future pace.

Purpose of the Process:

This process is used to identify the differences between the visual, auditory, kinesthetic, olfactory and gustatory submodalities in a problem state and a desired state. The submodalities of the desired state are then applied, one-by-one, to the problem state.

Fictional Treatment:

Our language is peppered with metaphors of transformation: "Dross into gold." "Silk purse from a sow's ear." "Water into wine." "March comes in like a lion and goes out like a lamb." Submodalities have the power to transform a problem state into a desired state, one element at a time.

Look to the natural world for inspiration and practice in describing routine (yet no less miraculous) transformations. Consider the submodality changes that occur in the following:

–   Day and night.

–   A blooming garden and fallow ground.

–   A growing child.

–   The seasonal changes in trees or lakes or birds.

When dealing with the problem state - that which is to be transformed - describe it in as much sensory-based detail as possible. Besides making for more interesting reading, this accomplishes several things. It gives you an opportunity to involve all five senses. It will also make it easier to identify the "drivers," those submodalities provide the most profound level of change, making a more defined contrast between the problem state and the desired state.

As the storyteller, you have the power to transform characters and objects. When dealing with people, it is the characteristics of their undesired behavior that are most important to emphasize. Keep your descriptions sensory based. What are your characters seeing, hearing, feeling, smelling[6] and tasting while in their "stuck state." What are their actions, words and thoughts? Here you have an opportunity to violate the Meta Model principal of "mind reading." Go ahead and read your characters' minds. What is their internal dialogue? What is their perception of themselves and their environment?

The desired or "post-transformation" state should be described in an equal amount of detail. Keep the context the same or similar to emphasize the differences between the present state and the desired state. If someone is afraid when they are alone in a dark, quiet room and then become resourceful in the bright sunshine, surrounded by friends, it doesn't make for a meaningful transition because the context is so drastically different.

When writing about objects, focus on the descriptions of their unique characteristics. How do you know that a bunny rabbit is a bunny rabbit, or that a pickle is a pickle? What unique attributes do they have that, if changed, would make them something completely different?

Enact your transformations one element at a time, rather than "P-O-O-F - all fixed!" It gives your audience a chance to savor each change; to see, hear, feel, taste and smell the differences in their own imaginations. It draws out the process and provides for some anticipation of reaching the desired state. Create suspense. Tease out the changes. Dole them out like sweets.

When dealing with characters (rather then objects) resist the temptation to use an outside catalyst as a change agent. Any transformation that is the result of a fairy godmother, magic wand or enchanted lamp will be hollow and superficial, robbing your characters and your audience of the opportunity to feel satisfied and empowered by the change. The subconscious is magical and has greater powers than any contrived device that you could use.

You will be giving your characters the power to create their own reality using submodality changes, which is what we do in real life anyway. A frightful memory isn't neutralized because it **literally** becomes farther away or dimmer. We merely **perceive** it as being different and so it is.

_____

[6]Don't underestimate the olfactory sense. It is the most powerful memory stimulus of all the senses and is also the only one that bypasses critical analysis and goes directly to the limbic system - the emotional center of the brain.

THE DREAM PILLOW

Somewhere to the north in a mountainous land with harsh winters and mild summers, there lived a warrior king who had a magical pillow. If he slept upon the pillow and dreamed about something, he could change it into whatever he wanted. The pillow had been a gift from a passing peddler he jailed for not paying the proper tax on his wares. Upon the peddler's release after serving the required thrice thirteen days, he handed the pillow to the warrior king and said, smiling, "Be careful what you desire in your dreams."

If the warrior king dreamed about an ordinary rock, he could change the rock into pure gold, which he would use to buy food and ammunition for his armies. If he dreamed about a plain, dull kitchen knife, he could transform it into a jewel handled sword, which he would use to fight his enemies. And if he dreamed about a field mouse, it would become mighty stallion, which he would ride into battle.

The warrior king had everything he wanted. He would ride for miles about his kingdom and admire all he ruled. He would glory in the victory of battle. He would sit in his vaults and count all his money. As the years passed, however, he began to notice an emptiness that could not be filled with the thrill of a victorious and bloody defeat of his enemies, or the acquisition of lands by force, or the accumulation of wealth from taxing his subjects.

"I must take a wife and she will bear me a son," he thought, "and that will surely fill this emptiness inside me." He set about immediately to choose a suitable bride. It couldn't be just any woman. It had to be someone who would live up to the responsibility as the wife of a great warrior king. She must be strong, wise, healthy, virtuous and beautiful.

The king sent messengers in six directions to look for her, with instructions to return in twice thirteen days, having located the appropriate candidate, for a prize of an ounce of gold. The messengers set off on fast horses and the king went about his business of ruling and fighting and judging and imprisoning and taxing, and all the other tasks that befall a warrior king who is largely indifferent to the welfare of his subjects.

A messenger returned in thirteen days, flush with the news of his discovery and eager for his prize. He was so breathless with excitement that he could barely speak. "Her name is Neola and she is everything the you asked for and more," he said. "She is wise and strong and healthy and virtuous and very, very beautiful."

The warrior king was elated and gladly gave the messenger his reward. He put on his best armor, readied his best riding mare and began his journey to his future wife. He arrived at Neola's door, flanked by lieutenants and servants, with fanfare and pomp.

Neola greeted the king cooly, for his reputation as a ruthless warrior and unsympathetic ruler has widely known. She had always promised herself that she would marry for love and had no intention of going off with this arrogant man to live as his wife. She also knew that he was accustomed to getting what he wanted, by any means necessary.

The warrior king got right down to business, saying, "I have come here to claim you as my wife. I have many fine lands and great wealth. You will bear me a son and he will take over my kingdom. You will be well treated and will live a life of ease and comfort. You will have servants and fine clothes."

Neola listened closely to his words and watched the expression on his face, and she knew that this man's heart was hard, that he took what he wanted and used it as he saw fit and that he would never love her the way she needed to be loved. However, she also feared giving him an outright refusal, for she had no doubt that a rejection would bring violence on her house.

An idea came to her. "I will marry you," she said, "if you bring me four gifts in four days, and if I find those gifts acceptable."

The warrior king agreed immediately, for he had brought with him the finest things from his land to offer to his bride-to-be. "I'll return tomorrow with your first gift and the courtship will begin."

Of course, Neola had no intention of finding any of the gifts acceptable.

The warrior king returned the next day with a peach, golden and sweet. He handed it to Neola and as he did, her fingertips grazed his hand; it was cold and rough. She shivered inside and slowly turned the peach over and over in her hands, looking at it thoughtfully. She handed it back to the warrior king and said, looking him straight in the eye, "Thank you, but I would rather have a lemon. A peach you just eat and, although it is delicious, it is quickly gone." "A lemon," she said, "I can slice and use to season many fine dishes, then dry the peal to flavor the cider this winter."

The king was visibly annoyed at Neola's insolence, but he was willing to live up to his side of the bargain. Besides, Neola did not know about his dream pillow, so bringing her a lemon the next day would be easy. So he took the peach with him and promised to return the next day.

That night, he slept upon his dream pillow and dreamed about the peach. While he slept, the peach began to change. The large, hard stone became tiny, soft seeds. The firm flesh became thousands of tiny sections. The delicate fuzz on the skin became hard, dimpled rind. And, the sweet fragrance and taste became sharp and tangy and salty.

The warrior king awoke to find that the peach had become a lemon and he smiled.

He went again to Neola's house with the lemon and a beautiful, tiny bird in a bamboo cage. Neola thanked the warrior king for the lemon and slipped it into her pocket. She was somewhat surprised that he had been able to find one so quickly, but she did not let it show on her face.

The warrior king then gave her the bird and she held the cage up and looked inside at the small creature. Again, to the king's amazement, she handed it back to him. "Thank you. However, I would really rather have a cricket because they bring good luck and are not so noisy or difficult to care for."

The king left, cage in hand, and rode sullenly back to his lodgings. "She is asking a lot of my patience," he thought. "But, it will be worth it when she is my wife and bears me a fine son to take over my kingdom."

That night, the king slept on his dream pillow and dreamed of the tiny bird. While he slept, the bird began to change, its feathers faded away and a hard skin appeared. Its sharp beak became a blunt snout. Its tuneful singing changed to a high pitched chirping.

The warrior king awoke to find that the bird had become a cricket and he smiled.

He set off for Neola's home with the cricket and thirteen red roses to offer her as her third gift. Neola greeted him politely and thanked him for the cricket. She was surprised that he had located one so quickly, because crickets were so difficult to catch. But, she calmly accepted the roses from him and looked at them carefully. She could smell their sweet perfume and feel the thorns pressing into her hands. She handed them back to a very surprised king and said, "Thank you. But, I'd really rather have some garlic. Roses are beautiful, but they fade and then you are left with nothing. Garlic keeps away a cold and flavors the meat and it lasts for months."

The king could barely conceal his rage as he left with the roses. He held them so hard, the thorns cut into his skin. He rode back to his lodge, thinking, "She is the most ungrateful woman I have ever met!"

That night, the king slept on his dream pillow and dreamed of the roses. While he slept, their color changed from bright red to milky white. The soft, velvety petals became firm cloves, covered with a thin, papery skin. Their sweet fragrance changed to a savory, pungent aroma.

The warrior king awoke to find that the roses had changed to garlic and he smiled.

He started toward Neola's house with the garlic and a bolt of silk cloth. Neola accepted the garlic and cloth. She looked at the silk closely and ran her hand over the smooth, soft surface of the fabric. She handed the bolt of silk back to him and said, "Thank you, but I would rather have wool. Silk is beautiful, but not very practical. Wool is sturdier and more versatile. Please bring me a bolt of wool."

This time, the king could not contain his anger. "This is the finest silk in all the land! It cost a hundred gold pieces and one of my best horses!"

"Just the same," said Neola, "I would rather have wool."

The king turned on his heel, clutching the silk in angry hands and stomped out to his horse. He rode back to his lodging, muttering under his breath. "No matter," he said to himself, "tonight I will dream of the silk, and its fine, shiny texture will change to a course grain. It will become thicker and heavier and denser. And, when I awaken, it will be a bolt of wool and then she will have to marry me."

That night, when he returned to his lodgings, the frustrated warrior king fell asleep on his dream pillow. In his fitful dream, he looked everywhere for the bolt of silk, but could not find it. He was in a hall of mirrors and all that he could see was himself. And so, while he slept, his hard heart began to soften. His cold hands began to warm and become sensitive again. He harsh, loud voice became lower and more mellow. His smile, once a grimace of triumph and cruelty, widened and the muscles in his rigid face relaxed.

When the warrior king awoke the next morning, the bolt of silk was still a bolt of silk.

He sat in the window of his lodge and watched the sun rise and he smiled.

Recap of Story:

Write down which plot elements, dialogue or characters you think fulfill each of these steps of the process (See Chapter 17 for the author's recap).

1.   Identify a problem state.

_____

2.   Identify an appropriate resource state.

_____

3.   Identify the differences between the visual, auditory and kinesthetic submodalities of each state.

_____

4.   Map across by keeping the same content and changing the modalities one at a time.

_____

5.   Test and future pace.

_____

FAMILY RECIPE

Mom-mom stomped her size twos on the floor, thereby demanding the attention of the entire clan. Everyone stopped what they were doing and listened, and while they listened they looked for shelter - the nearest piece of furniture to duck behind in case of incoming. Mom-mom was tiny and old, but her throwing arm got stronger every year. A piece of toast or a wet dish cloth became weapons of destruction in her weathered hands. She had once hit Uncle Row in the eye with a buttermilk biscuit when he did not show the proper appreciation for her cream gravy. He was cross-eyed for three days.

"Now listen up, you," said Mom-mom. "The wedding gumbo is in the pot. The kitchen is hereby off limits for the next twenty-four hours except for me. Is there anyone here who does not understand what I'm telling?" Mom-mom accepted the silence that followed as complete and total understanding, which it was.

Wedding gumbo was a serious matter in the Mackajon family. It was a recipe handed down from seven generations past and a traditional meal at every family nuptial since before the Civil War. Legend had it that the original recipe was written on the back of Great Uncle Lambert's conscription papers with a sharp pine stick and iodine. Mom-mom claimed to have it hidden away somewhere, but would never show it to anyone.

Now that Jordy was engaged to the Plowdish girl, it was time for another batch of gumbo. Mom-mom would use a kettle the size of a wheelbarrow and stay up for twenty-four hours cooking it, not letting anyone come near the kitchen for fear they'd add something or see something or ask something she didn't want them to. Bad thing was, Mom-mom was not that great a cook. Good thing was, Mom-mom hadn't been able to stay up for twenty-four hours for long, long time.

Round dusk, the house fell quite and one-by-one family members snuck past the kitchen to listen for Mom-mom's raspy snoring. Once Mom-mom was asleep, the gumbo began to change.

Aunt Bubba June was the first one to creep, sock footed, into the kitchen and lift the lid off the pot. "Land," she thought, "Mom-mom hasn't even turned the burner on." She quietly turned the knob on the stove and held her hand against the pot. When the cold, smooth steel began to warm and then get hot, she smiled. "Now, at least the darn stuff'll cook." She stole up the stairs and into bed.

Patsy quietly opened the screen door from the sleeping porch and slipped into the kitchen. Mom-mom's snoring sounded like sandpaper on tree bark so she was safe. She lifted the lid of the gumbo pot and a sharp acidic smell curled her toes. "Ouiiee!" she whispered to herself. "Mom-mom knows good and well that when you cook with okra, you got to put in some lemon juice or you've got yourself a sour pot of something not fit for hounds or hobos," she thought.

She took two lemons from the windowsill and silently sliced them in half. She squeezed the juice into the pot, wiped her hands and stirred. The acrid smell was transformed into a savory fragrance. Patsy closed her eyes and inhaled, holding the scent and smiling. "That's how gumbo should smell," she thought. She glanced at Mom-mom slumped in the kitchen chair asleep and then stole back to the sleeping porch with a self-satisfied smile.

Next came Iris, with a spoon hidden in her robe pocket. She silently lifted the lid of the huge pot and dipped the spoon in the gumbo. Tasting it, she rolled her eyes in knowing confirmation. "I knew it," she thought. "Mom-mom always over does the maple sugar and under does the cayenne." It all came from the time when she had been a little too generous with the cayenne back when Uncle Bayliss got married. The preacher had two helpings before the fire took hold and he had to keep ice cubes in his mouth all that day and into the night. The whole thing caused quite a ruckus and it was the talk of Elbow Holler for months afterward. It shied Mom-mom up a little. Iris got the jar of cayenne and sprinkled some into the pot. She stirred the gumbo and tasted again. The cloying sweetness had changed to a rich, peppery blend of flavors. The perfect balance of maple sugar and cayenne. Iris snuck back upstairs to her room.

Glancing around for any activity and with one eye on Mom-Mom, Uncle Japeth picked up the pot lid and looked at the gumbo. "Well dirty darn," he thought, "that fool old lady **never** puts in enough file." The broth was clear and Japeth could see right through to the bottom of the pot where the big ham bone rested. He quietly rummaged through the pantry and found the file box. He shook in a goodly helping - enough to thicken that broth and give that stuff some body - he hated a thin gumbo. He slowly stirred and watched as the broth became cloudy, thickened and then turned completely opaque. "Now," thought Uncle Japeth, "you should be able to walk across that stuff in full hunting gear!" He checked to see that Mom-mom was still asleep and snuck down the hall to his room.

Dawn the next morning rolled across the horizon cool and dewey. Perfect wedding weather. Jordan Turnbull Mackajon was lawfully wedded to Mamie Alberta Plowdish surrounded by friends, family and neighbors. Afterward, there was music and food, dancing and food and presents and food. And, there was Mom-mom Mackajon's famous wedding gumbo - the best batch she ever made. She said so herself and not one person disagreed.

Recap of Story:

Write down which plot elements, dialogue or characters you think fulfill each of these steps of the process (See Chapter 17 for the author's recap).

1. Identify a problem state.

    _____

2. Identify an appropriate resource state.

    _____

3. Identify the differences between the visual, auditory and kinesthetic submodalities of each state.

    _____

4. Map across by keeping the same content and changing the modalities one at a time.

    _____

5. Test and future pace.

    _____

CHAPTER 11

PHOBIA/TRAUMA PROCESS

Summary of the Process:

1.   Access and calibrate the phobic state.
2.   Establish dissociation.
3.   Run a black and white movie of the event.
4.   Run the movie backwards.
5.   Test and future pace.

Purpose of the Process:

This process is used to neutralize a reaction to any traumatic experience or unpleasant response to a stimulus, including post-traumatic stress syndrome and physical abuse.

Fictional Treatment:

Establish your hero's phobic response by accessing the state. This can be done through memory alone or being re-exposed to the trigger event. Give your audience the opportunity to calibrate the hero by providing a good description of his reaction. This will be important later, when the hero is tested. You will want your audience to get a clean sort between the problem state and the desired state so that they are sure of how different your hero will be **after** the transformation is complete.

Consider your hero's environment and what might be a consistent enough reminder of the trauma to affect him on a fairly regular basis. (Someone could be phobic around solar eclipses or meteor showers, but those events probably don't occur regularly enough to compromise the quality of their lives.)

After you have established your hero's phobic or traumatic response, establish a dissociation. When doing a direct process, a "three place" dissociation is established in an abundance of caution. I don't think it's necessary to go that far in your story, unless it works well in your plot. The reason for a three-place dissociation in a direct intervention is to protect the client from re-living any past trauma, which is not as much of a consideration for your audience. Fictional treatment itself can be considered a "one-place" dissociation.

Consider some ways to separate your hero from her trauma, or the memory of it:

–   Time.

- Speed.
- Distance: height, perspective, looking through a telescope.
- Dusk, sunrise - other transitions of darkness and light.
- Walls, structures, barriers.
- Looking through windows.
- Water.
- Smoke.
- Weather of all sorts: fog, rain, snow, hail - anything that obscures vision.

The next step of the process will be a challenge for you to work into a story line: running a black and white movie of the event, then running the movie backwards. You can really have some fun with this, because your story might occur in a time or place where movies don't exist. You could have your hero imagine the event and then run it backwards much like the actual process, but stretch yourself and use some literary license. Consider the purpose of these two steps in the process: to create a less-than-vivid representation of the traumatic event and then to neutralize its effect.

How else could you represent the sequence of events that caused the trauma so that they can be reversed or otherwise obscured for your hero? Consider the following:

- Your hero is looking at an album of black and white photographs or drawings and then flips the pages backwards.
- The event is drawn - by your hero or someone else - in black ink and then it runs when exposed to water. Or, it is drawn with charcoal and then smeared.
- The event is represented by sticks, toothpicks or other objects which can be swept away.
- The event is drawn in the sand and washed away by the sea.
- The event is represented by some art form of your hero's creation. Consider the many works of art that are born of human suffering. The artistic process is therapeutic in and of itself. Is your hero a sculptor, dancer, singer, actor, writer or painter? Once created, how can the art be "reversed" or otherwise transformed to substitute for running the movie backwards?

Your goal here is to represent the sequence of events visually and then establish a means to sufficiently obscure or neutralize the memory for your hero, which has to occur naturally within the context of the story. This will be a challenge, so don't hamstring yourself by attempting to follow the process to the letter.

Once the phobia or trauma has been neutralized, test your hero by re-exposing her to the triggering event. Take the opportunity to show and tell your audience how different her response is. What else changes in her life? Future pace by hinting at what adventures might lay ahead for your hero now that this fear has been resolved. What has she been avoiding that she can now face with confidence?

LIGHTS OUT

It was the smell of metal, earth, ancient rocks and roots, that got her scared. She knew it was just ozone from the lightening's electrical charge that filled the hot air. Josie still stayed in her room as everyone else gathered on the porch to watch those scrawny fingers of lightening reaching from heaven to earth. They hooted and hollered, liked they'd won the lottery or shot a possum.

When it was all over and the electric lights began to glow and buzz again, Josie would wander down the stairs, acting aloof but with her heart still racing. "You should have seen her, Josie, it was a show and half," the family would tell her. They would all try and convince her that she had missed something important.

During the storms Josie felt more kinship with the machines in the house than the people. The television and radio, the fans and the light bulbs reacted just like she did. They sputtered, flickered, hesitated and then just plain shut down. They didn't rush out on the porch to see the show. They stayed inside, just like Josie stayed in her room.

One night, just after her birthday in late July, a doozie came around the mountain range, rumbling loud enough to rattle the fillings in everyone's teeth. Josie knew this one just might do her in and she ran to her room. Up two flights of stairs and behind the mahogany door that Grampy had built, she was safe. It was dark and the sounds were muffled. "If I put my head under the pillow, with Aunt May's quilt over top," she thought, "I can just about ride out the storm without crying.

Then she remembered a little science book she had had as a child. It was all about the weather. She dug through her old trunk, tossing out bundles of letters and old school art projects until she found the little book. She turned to the part about lightening and flipped the pages backwards, sending those jagged fingers back into the sky. She did it again and again, faster each time and eventually, the lightening didn't look so scary, going back up into the dark clouds where it belonged.

She put the little book back in her trunk and waited out the storm. It passed soon enough and the damage was bad. Willows laid flat on the ground and oaks just snapped because they were too stiff and somber. Boats moored on the creek landed in the center of town, looking lost and lonely. At least no one had been hurt.

While the rest of the family picked up debris from the yard, Josie unplugged machines, replaced fuses and got the household running again. She turned the radio on just in time to hear that another storm was headed their way. "This time," she thought, "I just might stay in the kitchen."

Recap of Story:

Write down which plot elements, dialogue or characters you think fulfill each of these steps of the process (See Chapter 17 for the author's recap).

1.   Access and calibrate the phobic state.

_____

2.   Establish dissociation.

_____

3.   Run a black and white movie of the event.

_____

4.   Run the movie backwards.

_____

5.   Test and future pace.

_____

DECISIONS, DECISIONS

If there were more than two choices, it was a crisis for Allen. Left or right was okay. Paper or plastic was fine. Democratic or Republican was do-able, as long as you left out the Green Party, the Libertarians, the Socialists, the Communists, etc. etc. Two was the maximum number of choices that Allen could deal with at any one time.

Most of the time he could put people off. He could get in his car, drive home, lock his doors and think about things. Then, he could get back to people. If he only had time to himself, time to think, time to sort out all the possibilities, he could manage. If he was put on the spot, he would wither like an orchid on a hot sidewalk. He would have to breathe through his nose while the sweat ran down his scalp and into his collar.

As Allen drove home from work, he thought, "If I can go back to where it had started, I could figure it out." He began to remember his high school debate team national championships. He had stared at the list of categories: extemporaneous, impromptu, serious interpretation, humorous interpretation, one-on-one debate, team debate. The list seemed endless and the championship was hanging in the balance. He had said, too loud, "Extemp!" It was his weakest category and he knew it. The coach sighed. His team mates rolled their eyes. He had lost badly and they had gone home empty handed.

At a stop light, he shut his eyes and imagined the tournament in scenes like still shots from a story board he had seen at a movie studio. When he went through them one by one, it didn't seem so overwhelming. He played them backward this time, a little faster and felt even better. Then he really zoomed through it in his mind and it was just a blur.

Allen sighed and felt that hard ball that had been in his stomach for so many years loosen up a little. He noticed he was hungry and wondered what he should take home for dinner. Chinese? Burritos? Thai? Pizza? It all sounded pretty good to him.

Recap of Story:

Write down which plot elements, dialogue or characters you think fulfill each of these steps of the process (See Chapter 17 for the author's recap).

1. Access and calibrate the phobic state.

   _____

2. Establish dissociation.

   _____

3. Run a black and white movie of the event.

   _____

4. Run the movie backwards.

   _____

5. Test and future pace.

   _____

Chapter 12

STORIES FOR CHILDREN

One of my favorite movies of all time since I was a tiny girl is *The Parent Trap*. I still watch it every time I am feeling a little bit blue, and it always cheers me up. It has been an ongoing source of comfort for me that I have been at a loss to explain and have been teased about greatly. Seeing it in my video collection, a friend recently commented that it was the ultimate conflict integration story. I had to agree: Twin girls separated as babies - each unaware that the other exists. One is street smart, one book smart and they **hate** each other on sight. In fact, it is their very likeness that makes them bitter enemies. Of course, they come to realize how much they need each other to create what each cannot create on their own: a family.

Why is it that I watch *The Parent Trap* over and over, and that I especially want to watch it when I'm upset or lonely? Why is it that little kids want to hear the same story so many times it makes their parents crazy? We can entertain all sorts of literary and psychological theories about epic themes and archetypes, but I think the reason is more basic: the words have a certain rhythm, we identify with the characters, and we look forward to our favorite parts of the story and a happy ending. We can drift off to sleep knowing that all is well in our universe. In a world where things are often unpredictable and sometimes a little scary, those familiar, soothing stories can be a tremendous source of comfort to the child in all of us.

When my husband's nieces and nephews were small, there were certain family "camp fire stories" that they wanted to hear again and again. Every time the clan gathered for a holiday, one of them would pipe up with, "Tell us about the time that Uncle Paul drove the tractor into the cranberry bog!" They heard this and other stories dozens of times, but they never tired of them.

The re-telling of those tales connected them to their roots and gave them the opportunity to picture the adults in the family as children like themselves. They knew that since Uncle Paul was there to celebrate Thanksgiving, he must have survived the ordeal. Knowing this made it safe to for them to really get into the story. They could picture Uncle Paul at fifteen years old, teetering on the brink of the cranberry bog in a rogue tractor. They could afford to get scared with him and for him, to live the story rather than just listen to it.

The oral tradition of storytelling has been replaced by visual media, and many of us are starved for stories that teach us the wisdom of our elders and reconnect us to a larger system - clan, family, race, tribe, species. If there are children in your family - of any age - it would be a great gift to tell stories that not only entertain, but that teach and heal as well.

Consider your favorite fairy tales, stories or movies and look at them through new eyes - hear them with new ears. Do they represent or include integration? Transformation? Reframing of a negative situation? Someone who changes their future by changing the way they perceive their past? Some elements of NLP processes are probably present in the stories that you find most inspiring, comforting or entertaining.

Consider what would it be like to re-tell some classic fairy tales with an NLP perspective:

Chicken Little told as a phobia/trauma process. Chicken Little is scared out of his wits because an acorn fell on his head, so he runs amok in the barnyard, trying to stir up the rest of the livestock. (Perhaps you know people like this.) His mother takes him up into the hayloft where he can watch through the window and over the fence **(two place dissociation)**. He can see that it was just an acorn that fell on his head and not the sky.

Little Red Riding Hood told as a swish process. The Big Bad Wolf swallows Little Red Riding Hood whole, so she's apparently down in his stomach in a little ball **(present state)**. When the woodsman cuts open the Big Bad Wolf, Red jumps out - alive and fine as can be. The "wonderful" Red springs to full size **(desired state)** while the Big Bad Wolf falls back dead **(cue image overtaken by the desired state or "wonderful self" image)**.

Jack and the Beanstalk told as a change personal history process. This may be a little more of a stretch, but consider what Jack did by trading the milk cow **(present state)** and getting the magic beans **(resources)** which grew into the beanstalk that lead him to the goose that laid the golden eggs **(desired state)**. Jack changed his family's future by letting go of the past and using new resources.

The Three Little Pigs told as a parts integration process. The pigs all start out in separate houses, each thinking that they will be safe from the wolf with only their own resources, but eventually they all end up in the safest place, the brick house **(recognizing the positive intent and advantages that each one has to offer)**, and together they trick the Big Bad Wolf and save each other by combining their resources and working together

Goldilocks and the Three Bears told as mapping across kinesthetic submodalities process. Goldilocks shows up at the bears' cottage hungry and tired **(present state)**. The porridge is too hot or too cold. The bed is too hard or too soft. But, Goldilocks persists **(shifting submodalities)** until she finds a bowl of porridge and a bed that are "just right" and she is full and comfortable **(desired state)**.

Have some fun by exploring your favorite children's stories: open your awareness to the use of NLP processes in them and notice how it adds to the creative tension of the plot, enhances the identity of the characters and carries the story forward. Compare these stories to the Model for the Well Formed Story to gain an understanding of how each of the elements work and familiarize yourself with the techniques to gain mastery in your own storytelling.

Consider how you might retell an old favorite or a classic tale by weaving in the steps of an NLP process. Don't feel like you must include each of the steps in their exact order. Even telling a little story or offering a conversational metaphor that contains a simple reframe or submodality shift can be very powerful.

CHAPTER 13

FOUND MYTHOLOGY

My husband and I play a game while we're waiting at airports for our flight, or in restaurants for our food to come. We'll pick someone out of the crowd and take turns making up their history, what they do for a living, etc. One Christmas Eve, we were having a lovely buffet dinner at the Fairmont Hotel in San Francisco. We picked out a gentlemen a few tables away and began discussing what each of us thought he did for a living. We actually called him over to our table and asked him. As it turned out, we were both wrong, but he was quite amused at being the subject of our guessing game.

The makings of myth and storytelling are all around you. Slow down and pay attention to the characters in your life, especially the ones you only see from a distance and never really get to know. Study them. Imagine what their life is like, where they come from, who loves them, what they eat for dinner, what makes them cry. Let your imagination run wild. Pick one thing about someone you encounter on the street (their socks don't match) and see how far you can carry that into a story.

Look around your neighborhood, your work, the park across the street, the coffee shop. Your world is teeming with characters; just pick one and build a story around them:

- The dentist with a tooth missing.
- The neighbor that looks like she could be royalty fallen on hard times.
- The elderly woman who carries hundreds of plastic bags stuffed into another plastic bag.

Go into an antique store or second hand shop in your neighborhood and find something that catches your eye:

- Who was the first person that owned this?
- Who was the last?
- What was the journey that brought it to this place?
- If it was imbued with magical powers, what could it do?

Listen to conversations around you. I was once in a restaurant and overheard someone from the next table say, "We had to wait until it rained so we could initiate the newcomers." I thought to myself, "There's definitely a story behind that." Listen between the lines. What **aren't** people saying? What's missing? Get quiet and focus on one noise a time; isolate individual sounds. Ask yourself:

-     Why is it that the only third step in your apartment building squeaks; what happened there long ago?

-     Who is in the first car you hear drive by your house in the morning, and where are they going?

-     What would it be like of fish screamed when you pulled them out of the water?

-     What if babies had mastery of spoken language from their birth?

Our bodies are covered with a sensitive, complex sensing organ - skin. Dozens of objects that pass through our hands every day. How often do we really pay attention to what they feel like?

-     With your eyes closed, describe the difference between skin and plastic, an apple and an avocado, a marble and a cotton ball.

-     How would you explain what it feels like to take a hot bath to someone who's never had one?

-     Close your eyes the next time you hug a loved one - how do you know it's them?

Examine your own life and history. Everything that you have ever seen, heard, felt, smelled or tasted is stored in your memory. Think about pivotal times in your life; times when you either had massive change, growth, joy, loss or learning. Consider all the events and experiences that have made you the person you are today:

-     Where did your family come from?

-     What was the first song you ever sang?

-     What was your most triumphant moment? Your scariest?

-     Who was your best friend in third grade?

-     What's the worst meal you ever ate?

-     When was the last time you rode a roller coaster?

-     When you were a child, what did you want to be when you grew up and why?

-     What persons have influenced you the most?

-     What was your greatest lesson?

- Your most precious gift?

- Your fondest longing?

- Your deepest secret?

This is the time for fantasy, conjecture, creativity and daydreaming. Stare off into space and ask yourself:

- If I could live for twenty four hours in any movie I've seen, which one would it be?

- If I could spend a week living in any time in history, which one would I choose?

- If I could speak the language of any other animal on earth, which would I pick?

- If I could bring any inanimate object to life, what would it be?

- If I had to listen to the same song for twenty four hours straight, which one would I pick?

Spend time noticing the details around you. Consider daydreaming and fantasizing to be time well spent. Gather up your anecdotes and memories and use them all to craft your own well formed stories.

CHAPTER 14

THE PROOF OF THE TALE IS IN THE TELLING

Once you have written a story, don't just put in a drawer somewhere. Read it aloud to someone. Even better, read it enough times that you can tell it out loud. This leaves your hands free to gesture and allows you to make eye contact with your audience and to calibrate for their responses.

This may be a stretch for some of you. Make yourself do it anyway. The spoken word has magic, so send your story into the universe and notice what kind of miracles begin to happen. Give it voice and put it out there.

If you are truly shy, and mortified at the thought of reading your story aloud to someone, try the following:

– Record it and play it back for yourself.

– Climb a hill out in the forest and read it to a tree or some kindly squirrels.

– Tell it to yourself in the shower or in your car.

– Have it translated into a foreign language.

Find a group of sympathetic souls who also want to create mythology and tell stories with NLP and form a salon. Agree to meet once a month (or more) and tell your stories to each other. I guarantee you that you are your own worst critic and that releasing your creative force in the presence of like minded souls will do wonders for your storytelling and writing skills.

If you want someone to practice your storytelling on, hang around with children. They love to hear stories and they are so much more adept at suspending reality, and are far less critical, than grown-ups. They don't care about plot, point of view or character development. Most children would just like to have some kind attention from a caring adult.

Really punch it up for them: do different voices for each character, make sound effects, alter your pace and tonality to create moods. They will love it, and I promise you that they will return your efforts tenfold with their appreciation. Your confidence will soar and you'll be helping to revive the ancient oral tradition of passing on stories from one generation to the next.

Once, when my two cousins and I were small, we begged my uncle to read us a story. He was busy so he told us to go and ask my cousins' grandmother to read to us. Mor Mor was from

Sweden and spoke no English, so we were shocked that he would even suggest such an idea. "We can't understand a single word she says!" we cried. "Go and ask her anyway," he said. "It will make her feel good."

We reluctantly approached Mor Mor and asked her, without much enthusiasm, if she would please read to us from her book. Two hours later, my cousins and I were still sitting at her feet, intently following every musical syllable she spoke - totally enchanted and without one clue as to what she was saying. To this day, the sound of the Swedish language softens my heart and makes me feel like a child again.

CHAPTER 15

GLOSSARY OF NLP TERMS

Anchor   Any stimulus that evokes a response. Anchors can affect our *states*.

Associated   Being in an experience or memory as fully and completely as possible (with all the senses); perceiving from your own point of view.

Break State   To change someone's *state* dramatically. This is usually used to pull someone out of an unresourceful *state* or to create a neutral *state* between steps in a process.

Calibration   Accurately recognizing another person's *state* by reading non-verbal signals.

Congruence   Alignment of beliefs, values, skills and action. Being in *rapport* with oneself.

Dissociated   Experiencing an event or memory from any perspective other than your own point of view.

Ecology   Considering the effects of a change on the larger system instead of one isolated behavior, part or person.

First Position   Perceiving the world from your own point of view only. Being in touch with your own inner reality.

Future Pace   Rehearsing so that a person's behavior or set of behaviors becomes natural and automatic when prompted by the appropriate cues.

Kinesthetic   The feeling sense, tactile sensations and internal feelings.

Metaphor   Indirect communication by story or figure of speech, implying a comparison. Metaphors include similes, stories, parables, myths and allegories.

Neuro-Linguistic Programming   The study of the structure of subjective experience, a model of how individuals structure and express their experience.

Outcome   A specific, sensory-based desired goal.

Pacing   Gaining and maintaining *rapport* with another person by meeting them in their model of the world.

Presuppositions	Ideas or beliefs that are presupposed, i.e. taken for granted and acted upon.
Rapport	A relationship of trust and responsiveness with self or others.
Representational System	The different channels whereby we re-present information internally, using our senses: sight (visual), sound (auditory), feeling/touch (kinesthetic), smell (olfactory) and taste (gustatory).
Resources	Anything that can help you achieve an *outcome*, i.e. possession, people, skills and abilities, *states*, experiences, strategies, etc.
Second Position	Perceiving the world from another person's point of view and gaining understanding of their reality.
Sensory Acuity	The process of learning to make finer and more useful distinctions from the sensory information we get from the world.
State	The sum of our thoughts, feelings, emotions and physical and emotional energy.
Submodalities	The fine distinctions we make within each of our *representational systems*, the qualities of our internal representations.
Third Position	Perceiving the world from the viewpoint of a detached observer.
Trance	An altered *state* of consciousness resulting from an inward focus of attention.

Chapter 16

NLP PRESUPPOSITIONS FOR WRITERS

The following is an adaptation of the NLP presuppositions as they might be applied to storytelling and writing.

1.   I make maps of my own experiences by writing and telling stories.

2.   I can make my stories richer and fuller maps of experience by using language that appeals to all representational systems.

3.   My stories are not reality.

4.   People respond to my stories according to their maps of reality.

5.   My writing reflects any changes in my maps.

6.   My writing may reflect the fact that my maps that are sometimes out of my conscious awareness.

7.   Behind every story I write or tell, I have a positive intention.

8.   Having choice as a storyteller is preferable to not having choice.

9.   I write and tell the best stories I can given my skills, abilities, insight and resources.

10. The more flexibility I have as writer and storyteller, the more influence I will have on my audience.

11. I communicate as a writer in each representational system, even if I am not aware of it.

12. The meaning of my stories is the response they elicit from my audience.

13. I work perfectly to produce whatever results I achieve in my stories.

14. Each one of my writing skills and techniques is useful in some context.

15. I can write anything.

16. I can work through any block in my story by chunking it down in small enough pieces.

17. I already have all the resources I need to be an effective writer or storyteller (or, I know how to find those resources).

18. There is no such thing as a rejection letter, only a feedback letter.

19. The quality of my work as a writer is largely due to my ability to communicate to my audience.

20. My writing comes from a system that includes my mind and my body.

21. I have no inner enemies, although I may have an inner critic.

22. I can make positive changes in the quality of my writing abilities by adding resources.

Chapter 17

RECAP OF STORIES

CHAPTER 6 - SORTING POLARITIES/CONFLICT INTEGRATION:

<u>Phoebe and Philopena</u>

1.   Access two extreme parts that are in conflict.

    The girls, Phoebe and Philopena, after they have separated and are on their respective islands.

2.   Elicit the outcome of each in positive terms.

    To survive.

3.   Determine the advantages of each position.

    Each girl has enough food, shelter and water to survive on her island.

4.   Anchor the separation.

    Their separation is anchored first by the water between the islands, and then by their refusal to cross the spit of land and join one another.

5.   Obtain mutual appreciation of the positive outcomes and the advantages of each side.

    On the physical level, they discover that they have complementary materials with which to build a raft. On the emotional level, they realize how much they miss each other.

6.   Integrate the polarities, creating a balanced, unified whole.

    The two girls finally meet in the middle of the land spit and agree to join forces and build a raft.

7.   Future pace.

    As they sail for home, they consider their friendship and the tales they will tell their families.

<u>A Tale of Two Monkeys</u>:

1.   Access two extreme parts that are in conflict.

    The two tribes of monkeys.

2.   Elicit the outcome of each in positive terms.

    To have the bananas from the banana tree.

3. Determine the advantages of each position.

    The roots of the tree are on one side and the branches are on the other.

4. Anchor the separation.

    They are separated physically by the river, and because they are too selfish and stubborn to share the bananas.

5. Obtain mutual appreciation of the positive outcomes and the advantages of each side.

    If they learn to get along, they can save the banana tree.

6. Integrate the polarities, creating a balanced, unified whole.

    The two tribes of monkeys come together in celebration after their leaders reach an agreement.

7. Future pace.

    Not included specifically, but the two monkey leaders did promise the old elephant that they would get along in the future.

CHAPTER 7 - SIX STEP REFRAME

<u>After Hours At Mrs. Blaylock's Toy Store</u>:

1.   Identify unwanted behavior.

    Bubble Machine's constant spinning of his handle.

2.   Establish communication with the part that generates the unwanted behavior.

    Sock Monkey asks Bubble Machine about the behavior.

3.   Distinguish the behavior from the positive intention.

    Bubble Machine wants to be King of the Toys.

4.   Access "creative part" and generate alternative behaviors to satisfy the positive intention.

    N/A.

5.   Check ecology - determine if there are any objecting parts and if so, address their positive intent, generate new alternatives, etc.

    Bubble Machine assures his handle that he will be busy.

6.   Future pace.

    The toys look calmer to Mrs. Blaylock when she returns to the store the next morning.

<u>Self Reflection</u>:

1.   Identify unwanted behavior.

    Looking in mirrors.

2.   Establish communication with the part that generates the unwanted behavior.

    Wonders about his compulsion.

3.   Distinguish the behavior from the positive intention.

    Wants to make a good impression, to be competitive.

4.   Access "creative part" and generate alternative behaviors to satisfy the positive intention.

    Trusting his "brains, intuition, verbal agility."

5.   Check ecology - determine if there are any objecting parts and if so, address their positive intent, generate new alternatives, etc.

    Considers the fact that other executives might get some of the goodies, but that's okay.

6.   Future pace.

    In the light of true self reflection, he likes the way he looks.

CHAPTER 8 - VISUAL SWISH

<u>Max's Wall</u>:

1.   Find a cue image that is seen just before an unwanted behavior or reaction.

        The wall that is covered with mud.

2.   Break state.

        Sleep.

3.   Using positive submodalities, create a desired state image or "wonderful self" image.

        The wall brightly painted with happy scenes from Max's life.

4.   Shrink the desired state image of the wonderful you down to the size of a dot. Place the dot containing the desired state image or wonderful you on the center of the cue image. Imagine the cue image getting smaller and darker while, simultaneously, the dot image of the wonderful you gets larger and overwhelms the cue image.

        Only a small corner of the wall is visible until the wind and water wash all the mud away and the entire wall is visible.

5.   Repeat step 4.

        Max replays the scene over in his mind.

6.   Test and future pace.

        N/A.

<u>Keepsake</u>:

1.   Find a cue image that is seen just before an unwanted behavior or reaction.

        Her husband making garlic (in this case, there is also a cue sound (his tinkering with pots and pans) and a cue smell (the brine of the pickling solution).

2.   Break state.

        Her sneeze.

3.   Using positive submodalities, create a desired state image or "wonderful self" image.

        Their wedding picture.

4.   Shrink the desired state image of the wonderful you down to the size of a dot. Place the dot containing the desired state image or wonderful you on the center of the cue image. Imagine the cue image getting smaller and darker while, simultaneously, the dot image of the wonderful you gets larger and overwhelms the cue image.

        A small corner of their wedding picture is visible until she wipes away the dust and the entire picture is visible.

5. Repeat step 4.

    N/A.

6. Test and future pace.

    She smells the brine again, but this time her irritation is overwhelmed by the happy memories; she goes downstairs to help with the garlic.

CHAPTER 9 - CHANGE PERSONAL HISTORY

<u>The Silence of the Sea</u>:

1.   Identify and anchor a problem state (a troubling experience from the past).

   Melanie's memory of the fight that happened at the lighthouse (triggered whenever she sees the lighthouse).

2.   Identify and anchor a resource (one that would have made it possible for you to have had a more productive, positive experience in the past situation).

   Her ability to intervene and resolve conflicts.

3.   Integrate by taking the resource state back into the problem memory and relive that experience in a new way.

   She imagines how different the fight would have been if she had intervened.

4.   Test and future pace.

   Melanie decides to welcome the new tenants of the lighthouse.

<u>Cool Shade</u>:

1.   Identify problem state (a troubling experience from the past).

   His behavior at a recent difficult client meeting.

2.   Identify a resource (one that would have made it possible for you to have had a more productive, positive experience in the past situation).

   The ability to sit and listen quietly.

3.   Integrate by taking the resource state back into the problem memory and relive that experience in a new way.

   Seeing himself posed like the wise frog during the meeting.

4.   Test and future pace.

   Thinking ahead to when the next difficult situation arises and how different his behavior will be.

CHAPTER 10 - MAPPING ACROSS SUBMODALITIES

<u>The Dream Pillow</u>:

1.   Identify a problem state.

   This happens on two levels: first, the gifts are not acceptable and second, they warrior king is a hostile and lonely man.

2.   Identify an appropriate resource state.

   The specific gifts that Neola requests.

3.   Identify the differences between the visual, auditory and kinesthetic submodalities of each state.

   The differences between the peach and the lemon, the roses and the garlic, the bird and the cricket and the silk and the wool.

4.   Map across by keeping the same content and changing the modalities one at a time.

   This occurs in the warrior king's dreams.

5.   Test and future pace.

   The warrior king himself changes while dreaming and the morning finds him to be a new man.

<u>Family Recipe</u>:

1.   Identify a problem state.

   The gumbo will not turn out to be very tasty if Mom-Mom is left to her own devices.

2.   Identify an appropriate resource state.

   The additions each of the family members secretly make.

3.   Identify the differences between the visual, auditory and kinesthetic submodalities of each state.

   The differences between cold and hot, acidic and savory smell, too sweet and balanced taste and think broth and thick broth.

4.   Map across by keeping the same content and changing the modalities one at a time.

   This is done as each family members adds an ingredient while Mom-Mom sleeps.

5.   Test and future pace.

The gumbo turns out to be delicious - boding good fortune for the newlyweds.

CHAPTER 11 - PHOBIA/TRAUMA PROCESS

<u>Lights Out</u>:

1. Access and calibrate the phobic state.

   Josie is afraid of storms. We know that she may look calm, but her heart is racing.

2. Establish dissociation.

   Upstairs, behind a heavy door and under a quilt.

3. Run a black and white movie of the event.

   Flips the pages of her science book.

4. Run the movie backwards.

   Flips the pages backwards, sending the lightening back into the sky.

5. Test and future pace.

   Josie hears about another storm coming on the radio, and decides she can stay downstairs.

<u>Decisions, Decisions</u>:

1. Access and calibrate the phobic state.

   Allen is panicked by making decisions. He sweats and his stomach ties up in knots.

2. Establish a dissociation.

   Gets in his car, drives home and locks the doors.

3. Run a black and white movie of the event.

   Imagines the scene like pictures in a story board.

4. Run the movie backwards.

   Imagines the scene moving backwards.

5. Test and future pace.

   He easily contemplates choosing between several things for dinner.

RESOURCES AND REFERENCES

Andreas, Connierae, Ph.D. and Andreas, Steve, MA, *Heart of the Mind.* Moab, Utah: Real People Press, 1989.

Bandler, Richard & Grinder, John, *The Structure of Magic.* Palo Alto, California: Science and Behavior Books, Inc., 1975.

Bernays, Anne and Painter, Pamela, *What If? Exercises for Fiction Writers.* New York: HarperCollins, 1990.

Bierlein, J.F., *Parallel Myths.* New York: Ballentine, 1994.

Calvin, William H., *How Brains Think (Evolving Intelligence, Then and Now).* New York: BasicBooks, A Divsion of HarperCollins Publishing, Inc., 1996..

Campbell, Joseph, *The Power of Myth.* New York: Doubleday, 1988.

Cook, Marshall J., *How to Write with the Skill of a Master and the Genius of a Child.* Cincinnati, Ohio: Writers' Digest Books, 1992.

Grimm, Jakob and Wilhelm, *Grimm's Fairy Tales.* Garden City, New York: Junior Deluxe Editions, 1959.

Grinder, John & Bandler, Richard, *The Structure of Magic II.* Palo Alto, California: Science and Behavior Books, Inc., 1976.

Hadley, Josie and Staudacher, Carol, *Hypnosis for Change (A Practical Manual of Hypnotic Techniques).* Oakland, California: New Harbinger Publications, 1989.

Haley, Jay, *Uncommon Therapy (The Psychiatric Techniques of Milton H. Erickson, M.D.).* New York: W.W. Norton & Company, 1973, 1986.

Keen, Sam and Valley-Fox, Anne, *Your Mythic Journey (Finding Meaning in Your Life Through Writing and Storytelling).* Los Angeles: Jeremy P. Tarcher, Inc., 1973, 1989.

Larsen, Stephen, *The Mythic Imagination (The Quest for Meaning Through Personal Mythology).* Rochester, Vermont: Inner Traditions International, 1990, 1996.

Markova, Dawna, Ph.D., *No Enemies Within.* Berkeley, California: Conari Press, 1994.

Markova, Dawna, Ph.D., *The Open Mind (Exploring the 6 Patterns of Natural Intelligence).* Berkeley, California: Conari Press, 1996.

McVickar Edwards, Carolyn, *The Storyteller's Goddess (Tales of the Goddess and Her Wisdom from Around the World)*. San Francisco: HarperSanFrancisco, A Division of HarperCollins Publishers, 1991.

Metzger, Deena, *Writing for Your Life (A Guide and Companion to the Inner Worlds)*. San Francisco: HarperCollins Publishers, 1992.

O'Connor, Joseph & McDermott, Ian, *Principles of NLP*. London: Thorson's, 1996.

Overdurf, John & Silverthorn, Julie, *Training Trances (Multi-Level Communication in Therapy and Training)*. Portland, Oregon: Metamorphous Press, 1994, 1995.

Pinkola Estes, Clarissa, Ph.D. *Women Who Run With the Wolves (Myths and Stories of the Wild Woman Archetype)*. New York: Ballantine Books, 1992.

Vogler, Christopher, *The Writer's Journey (Mythic Structure For Storytellers & Screenwriters)*. Studio City, California: Michael Weise Productions, 1992.

ABOUT THE AUTHOR

Mary Shannon Campbell is a certified hypnotherapist and NLP Master Practitioner with a private practice in San Francisco. Her articles have been published in *Anchor Point, The Practical Journal of NLP*. Her work with business and organizations includes one-on-one coaching and presentation of workshops on topics including stress management, interviewing and candidate selection, business communication skills and team building.

CONFLICT INTEGRATION WORKSHEET

Access the two extreme parts that are in conflict:[7]

Symbol:_____

Symbol:_____

Elicit the positive intent of each part:

Symbol:_____

Symbol:_____

Determine the advantages each part has to offer:

Symbol:_____

_____

[7]There may be one symbol for the two parts, or a symbol for each part; the same is true for their positive intentions and the advantages of each part. I have included two spaces to write down symbols for each step, but either way is fine.

Symbol:_____

Obtain mutual appreciation of the positive outcomes and the advantages each side has that the other does not have, but needs:

Symbol:_____

Integrate the polarities, creating a balanced, unified whole, with elements that neither could produce alone:

Symbol:_____

Future Pace (Think of a time in your future when it will be an advantage to have this unified whole in your life):

Symbol:_____

SIX STEP RE-FRAME WORKSHEET

A behavior that you want to change (something you do, but don't want to do):

Symbol:_____

The part that generates the unwanted behavior:

Symbol:_____

The positive intention of that part:

Symbol:_____

The creative part of you that learns new things, comes up with new ideas, etc.:

Symbol:_____

(Optional) Any part(s) that might object to having new behaviors:

Symbol:_____

(Optional) The positive intention of the objecting part(s):

Symbol:_____

Future pace (A situation in the future when you want to use this new behavior):

Symbol:_____

VISUAL SWISH WORKSHEET

Find a cue image that is seen just before an unwanted behavior or reaction:

Symbol:_____

Create a desired state image of yourself being different, having already solved this problem:

Symbol:_____

CHANGE PERSONAL HISTORY WORKSHEET

Identify and anchor a problem state (a troubling experience from your past that still bothers you when you think of it):

Symbol:_____

Identify and anchor a resource (one that would have made it possible for you to have had a more productive, positive experience in the past situation):

Symbol:_____

Integrate the resource into the problem state (reliving the experience in a new way):

Symbol:_____

Future pace (think about a time you might encounter a similar situation and knowing that you have this new resource available to you):

Symbol:_____

MAPPING ACROSS SUBMODALITIES WORKSHEET

Identify a problem state:

Symbol:_____

Identify an appropriate resource state:

Symbol:_____

Future pace (think of a time in the future when you might be in a similar context):

Symbol:_____

PHOBIA/TRAUMA WORKSHEET

Access the phobic state:

Symbol:_____

Future pace (think of a time in when you might encounter a similar situation):

Symbol:_____